HOW TO WRITE REALISTIC DIALOGUE

HOW TO WRITE
REALISTIC DIALOGUE

Jean Saunders

ALLISON & BUSBY

First published in Great Britain in 1994 by
Allison & Busby
an imprint of Wilson & Day Ltd
5 The Lodge
Richmond Way
London W12 8LW

A catalogue record for this book is available from the British
Library

ISBN 0 74900 192 5

Typeset by TW Typesetting, Plymouth
Printed and bound in Great Britain by
Mackays of Chatham Ltd, Lordswood, Kent

CONTENTS

Chapter 1

PERSONALLY SPEAKING

'There's nothing worse than a boring book,' my father used to say. 'Whenever I go to the library for something to read, I put it to the test. I open my chosen book five times at random. If all the pages I see have a fair sprinkling of dialogue in them, then I'm pretty sure the story will be interesting.'

My father was not an academic, nor even highly educated in the accepted sense of the word, but he was an avid reader, and his words have always stuck in my mind. I have no idea if they were his own, or came from some more erudite source, but over the years I've found myself practising what he preached. And it works, as simple methods often do.

In starting this book with a short piece of dialogue, I have also tried to illustrate a point by deliberately bringing my father into your consciousness. I didn't merely state the fact that opening a book at random was quite a useful guide to the book's interest. Instead, I made it a personal statement, which allowed you into a corner of my father's mind. If you had ever been fortunate enough to meet him at some later date, you would have known something about him, simply because you 'heard' him say those words.

We all get to know each other far more readily when we begin to converse. A person may be dressed in the most expensive clothes imaginable, and look like the most glamorous film star, yet as soon as she opens her mouth to speak, she may be revealed as someone quite different. A newspaper article may contain masses of facts about a person's life, but the article immediately becomes more emotive and personal when actual quotes are included.

MARKET STUDY
Market study for the purpose of writing dialogue may not seem a necessary requirement to you. After all, you know how people speak and how they react to one another, and you know you must sprinkle your book with bits of dialogue now and then. . . .

If you are a new writer, who may just be embarking on writing short stories or novels, then you need to have an idea of both the layout of dialogue in fiction, and the style of each publication for which you want to write.

It's futile to send a sparkling piece of imaginative writing, peppered with the kind of emotional dialogue more usually seen in a romantic novel, to a science-fiction magazine. It's just as time-wasting to write a romantic novel laced with hard-bitten Western dialogue.

Such mistakes are obvious, but variations of them still occur in unpublished manuscripts – which is probably why so many of them remain unpublished. You can get away with a great many faults in style and grammar – and even in fact – if you have a sympathetic editor who considers you a born storyteller and likes your work well enough to ask you to rewrite.

You will never get away with dialogue which doesn't fit into the style of your story, your chosen magazine, or the genre of your novel, and which, even more importantly, doesn't fit perfectly into the mouths of your characters.

Market study is never a waste of time, and no one should rush into writing fiction without making a detailed analysis of each of their characters. Only then will the author have a very good idea of how each character is going to speak. Character traits and personalities can also play a very great part in defining speech and voices, and you have the added advantage of deciding exactly how those voices will 'sound'. And make no mistake about it, you need to 'hear' them to define them accurately.

Is your heroine a softly spoken Irish colleen, or a fast-speaking Cockney? Was your hero brought up in America, still retaining a hint of a flat Boston accent or a Mississippi drawl? Or is he French, with an alluring accent? These are the kind of things to be decided even before you begin putting words into your characters' mouths, because each item will not only determine the things that they say, but also the way that they say them.

Market study includes reading the type of fiction you want to write. In particular, it means following the format of magazine fiction with regard to how much dialogue is preferred in an average short story. Very few stories are published without any dialogue at all, and it has to be an exceptional story – and writer – to succeed in this format.

Of course it can be done. All the writing rules can be broken if you are a Guy de Maupassant or an O. Henry but, since most of us are not, it pays to stick fairly closely to the rules while you are learning your craft. But I don't think you ever do stop learning, and it's a very arrogant author who thinks he/she knows it all.

DIALOGUE OPENINGS

A novel that begins with dialogue has a deliberate hook for the reader. It automatically involves the reader with the character who is speaking, and if you can begin any story with a wonderful line of dialogue, then you also make a great leap into the reader's interest.

Obviously, this may not appeal to everyone, and it can also be a difficult thing to do, especially if you haven't defined your character too clearly in your own mind yet. But this is where the character-analysis list comes into its own. I can't emphasise enough the value of preparing the ground when it comes to creating characters. And high on the list of describing each of your characters, so that you know as much about them as you can, is the way they're going to speak.

There are arguments for and against beginning a novel or short story with a line of dialogue. Some writers suggest that not all genres are suited to beginning in that way. I believe it can be used in any kind of novel, giving it dramatic impact from the first line.

3

Maybe you think a science-fiction novel or a crime novel with opening dialogue wouldn't be as effective as a teenage novel beginning with a shock sentence from your aggressive boy 'hero' intending to break into a record shop, for instance. It can be an interesting exercise to look through the books on your own bookshelves to see how many authors have used the dialogue opening, and to what effect.

So much in writing depends on your own temperament and style, and on the opening you're trying to create. In the end, it's up to you whether or not you think it's a good way to begin an novel. I have used the technique a handful of times in various novels, and it's worth considering, since it plunges the reader straight into the mind of the person who's speaking.

Examples
From *Lady of the Manor* (Jean Saunders, IPC Magazines Ltd):

'You surely don't intend going through with this ridiculous idea, Rhoda!'

A question is immediately put into the reader's mind. What is the idea that Rhoda's questioner finds so ridiculous? Rhoda obviously doesn't think the idea in any way ridiculous, and will probably bristle at the slight to her intelligence. The reader doesn't yet know what it's all about, which makes her read on to find out. It's also a pretty sure bet that the writer has every intention of making Rhoda go through with her 'ridiculous' idea.

Such a beginning creates that vital sense of curiosity in a reader, which is the real value of the dialogue opening. It also shows Rhoda to be someone with an independent mind of her own. A lot of information about a character can be gleaned from a simple piece of dialogue such as this.

From *Blackmaddie* (Jean Innes, Zebra Books):

'I won't go,' I exclaimed furiously.

Novels that are written in the first person, as in this gothic one, can have an added piquancy when begun with dialogue. The reader is thrown straight into the heroine's frustration, seeing it from the inside. Where won't she go? Why won't she go? And who is trying to make her?

From *Moonlight Mirage* (Sally Blake, Macdonald):

'Set me down here a moment, coachman.'

A simple dialogue opening, this. Someone is arriving at their destination, but the message conveyed by the sentence is slightly more subtle than that. By the use of that one word 'coachman', the reader would guess that this is a novel set in a time other than the present. It is, in fact, the beginning of an historical romance.

From *A Royal Summer* (Sally Blake, Mills & Boon Masquerade):

'Naturally, if Sir George Greville proposes marriage to you, Rosalind, I shall expect you to give the gentleman a favourable answer,' Miles Cranbourne said, far too casually for it to be a genuine afterthought.

This opening holds all the promise of a full-blown clash of personalities. The heroine is not the speaker, but from the words her father uses, the reader will expect fireworks from her. Romantic heroines, even historical ones, are no longer portrayed as clinging violets who comply meekly with their parents' wishes without having a brain in their heads.

From *Nightmare* (Jean Saunders, Heinemann Pyramid Books):

'What if we get caught?' Jenny said.

In this teenage novel, the simple question from the girl

arouses the same question in the reader. It is intended to make her want to read on to see what the couple intend to do that's so daring, wicked, frightening or illegal.

In every case that I have quoted, the usefulness of the dialogue opening is to arouse that curiosity, to draw the reader into the novel and into the character's mind. All the openings were carefully constructed to get the best out of them.

Many well-known authors have used the technique of the dialogue opening. Among them are:

M. M. Kaye in *Shadow of the Moon*
Marie Joseph in *A Better World Than This*
Frederick E. Smith in *633 Squadron*
Wendy Perriam in *After Purple*
Frederick Nolan in *Blind Duty*
Michael Legat in *The Silk Maker*
Sarah Harrison in *The Flowers of the Field*
Elizabeth Buchan in *Light of the Moon*
Agatha Christie in *Death on the Nile*

Authors who prefer the more leisurely opening to a novel would probably find this too stark a method and, in the end, it's up to each author to decide whether or not it's the right way to begin his or her story. I have quoted its usefulness in a novel context, but also for short stories, where every word must count, it's a very useful way to get your readers immediately involved in the action.

The dialogue does not need to be prolonged in this instance, and it would be fatal to let an unknown character indulge in a long speech at the beginning of page one! It's merely a hook, to lure the reader into the story.

AVOIDING DIALOGUE THAT BORES
No author wants to be accused of writing boring dialogue and, no matter how clever your plot or realistic your characters, if your dialogue lets them down, the story just won't sell.

Long-winded dialogue, where the author tries too hard to

put in everything possible about a subject, in order to impress the reader, should be avoided. Conversely, brief, trite exchanges that tell the reader nothing at all about the characters won't work either. Above all, don't allow your characters to indulge in a lengthy and meaningless conversation just to pad out the pages and fill the required number. This device will soon make the readers as bored as the characters, and make them wonder why you ever invented these people in the first place.

Always listen to the dialogue you give to your characters. Give each character a voice that is as individual to each of them as their fingerprints. Listen to that voice every time you write their lines of dialogue, and get into the habit of saying it aloud, since this is a great help for you to identify with their speech. Or you might try recording scenes of dialogue on a tape-recorder to hear if they sound vibrant enough, or if they simply fall flat.

The actual words you give your characters to say will depend heavily on the people and situations you have invented. But always try to find the most emotive words you can for your characters to say, to lift them out of the ordinary and to make them memorable.

Not every final speech can be as fraught with meaning as Rhett Butler's, but imagine how flat the scene would have been if he had merely said, 'I don't care.' I have often wondered how many times Margaret Mitchell turned the words of her famous sentence around in her mind, and on paper, or said them aloud, before she got them exactly right.

It can be just as effective to use a line of dialogue to end your fictional work, though this technique is not used so often. But of all the lines of dialogue in any piece of fiction, those that you choose to begin and end with must surely rate among the most important. Make them count.

BASIC PRINCIPLES OF PUNCTUATION

Writers who are starting to write fiction for the first time may well find themselves confused when it comes to the basic principles of punctuation. Maybe you haven't consciously thought about it since leaving school. Many people come to writing later in life, perhaps as a part-time hobby, or a way of earning some pin-money. Creative writing has become a very enjoyable way of meeting other people with similar ideas, but for many of them the actual setting out of manuscripts is completely foreign.

As a new writer, you are entering into a very competitive world, and those who have a little more experience than you will be sending out their manuscripts in pristine condition, typed and double-spaced on one side of consecutively numbered A4 sheets of paper, and all beautifully presented. This is the accepted way.

Even more experienced writers don't always follow carefully the correct layout of dialogue and punctuation. In many instances where I have judged writing competitions, this seems to be a grey area for many people, so for those who are still uncertain, I shall set out some of the basic principles.

There are not all that many layout rules for dialogue *per se*, but many manuscripts are submitted without knowing them or finding out about them. The layout seems to confuse a great many beginners, yet it is plain for anyone to see and follow, in any published magazine story or novel.

The most important thing to remember is to indent each new piece of dialogue when a character speaks, and always to enclose the 'speeches' in inverted commas, or quotation marks, to indicate where it begins and ends. Separating the dialogue from the prose makes for easier reading, and tells the reader who is now talking. Don't make the mistake of running on the dialogue of one person into the next, just because they only have a few words each to say.

Every time a character begins talking, you should indent that speech to begin a new paragraph. A character's section of dialogue may or may not be divided or 'supported' by the words 'he said', or other verbs or qualifications (which will be discussed later). If it is, then the speech on either side of 'he said' must be enclosed within more quotation marks, and the appropriate punctuation.

Note. If you choose to begin your paragraph with some *qualifying narrative* to the dialogue, then the paragraph may just as effectively begin with the narrative, thus:

> Mike turned back from the window. 'She should have returned by now,' he said.

Try to think of every speech, with all its relevant punctuation, as being enclosed in its quotation marks as if in a little box. Therefore, every comma, full stop, question mark or exclamation mark *that closes the speech* will also be enclosed inside that box, i.e. the quotation marks.

It is much easier to show the right and wrong methods than to explain them, so the following examples will illustrate this more clearly. In each case, the first sentence demonstrates the right way (√) to set out the piece of dialogue. The one immediately beneath it is the wrong way (×).

1. In the example below, the comma in (×) is wrongly outside the quotation marks.

> √ 'Move over,' he said.
> × 'Move over', he said.

2. You should not divide a speech that is being made by one person by including extra quotation marks after each sentence. Once you do this, it indicates that a second person is speaking, as in the following example. In (×) below, a reader would take it that two characters were commenting.

> √ 'You're in a hurry. Where's the fire?' Jack said.
> × 'You're in a hurry.' 'Where's the fire?' Jack said.

3. Each sentence of dialogue should end with the correct punctuation that the writer intends. This will make the reader pause in the correct place, or note that the sentence forms a question, or conclude that the speech has ended by the use of a full stop. A comma indicates that there is more to come.

9

The following piece of dialogue does not end with the word 'Odeon'. To continue the section, a comma is used to indicate that it closes with the words 'Mark said'.

    ✓ 'Why don't we go to a movie? There's a good one showing at the Odeon,' Mark said.
    × 'Why don't we go to a movie? There's a good one showing at the Odeon.' Mark said.

In example (×) above, the speech has been split and halted by the wrong use of a full stop after the word Odeon. 'Mark said' has become a complete sentence on its own, instead of an attribution.

4. In the following two examples, the use of the question mark and exclamation mark within each speech does not require a capital letter for the unnamed speaker. The capital letter gives emphasis to the word, which is not required in this instance. Again, it implies that 'She asked' and 'She snapped' are complete sentences, having nothing to do with what has gone before.

Saying these examples aloud will demonstrate the meaning further. Keep the voice low key when you say 'she asked' or 'she snapped', so that the dialogue flow of the entire speech is uninterrupted. Stressing the word 'She' in each case automatically makes you begin a new sentence. You subconsciously expect another piece of dialogue to follow.

    ✓ 'Shall we go together?' she asked.
    × 'Shall we go together?' She asked.

    ✓ 'I hate you!' she snapped.
    × 'I hate you!' She snapped.

5. Some people overdo the use of commas in sentences, while others virtually ignore them. Be warned that you can change the meaning of your sentence completely by putting a comma in the wrong place in the sentence. It can be disastrous, even hilarious, when this happens in dialogue.

Consider the following. The story has just involved a road accident, and a doctor is in attendance at the crash. A distraught woman passenger is trying to explain what happened.

    ✓ 'It was terrible, Doctor. With her car wheels spinning, Mary just lost all control.'
    × 'It was, terrible Doctor. With her car wheels, spinning Mary just lost all control.'

If she was spinning that fast, I'm not surprised ... and I'm not sure that the terrible Doctor is going to be all that much help either. The above example is an exaggeration, but shows how a dramatic scene can be completely ruined by inadvertently putting that comma in the wrong place. You need to 'hear' the sentence as you write it down, and to know when a speaking character would pause, and/or take a breath. Your reader needs to do that too, and your correct grammatical sentences should guide him or her.

Attribution to dialogue is a matter for the author to decide. In other words, which of these would you use?

        'Let's go out,' Mike said.
  or 'Let's go out,' said Mike.

Neither is wrong, and depends on your preference. It's not a bad idea to vary it occasionally, anyway. Similarly, the choice of putting double or single quotes around your dialogue is yours – unless your publishing house has a particular preference. The important thing is to be consistent throughout.

How do you punctuate a before-speech attribution? It can be done simply by the use of a comma, thus:

    Mike said, 'Let's go out.'

P. D. James uses a colon to separate the attribution from the dialogue, which to me, indicates a slightly longer pause than the old familiar comma. But can P. D. James be wrong? I think not, but this is another area of writing in which the author makes a personal choice. You could just as easily use a dash. If you are still undecided, then be guided by the style used in published fiction of the type you intend to write.

Personally, I don't care for too much before-speech attribution. I think it should be used sparingly, or it can become rather pretentious. But as an occasional variation to the other methods, it works admirably.

BRINGING CHARACTERS TO LIFE THROUGH DIALOGUE

In fiction, dialogue is essential as a means of getting to know the characters. If you doubt this, try to imagine reading a novel without any dialogue. The result would be a very lengthy piece of narrative, and whether it was composed largely of fast-moving action or the most beautiful descriptive passages, readers would soon get bored with it.

Dialogue brings characters to life more vividly than any other kind of writing, however dramatic or emotional. The quickest and best way to establish your characters is through their conversation with other people, so the sooner you can get your characters speaking in a story, the better.

As soon as you 'hear' them speaking, you feel that you know them. Relationships can be defined with the minimum of explanation, and the exchange of comments and opinions can say it all for you.

Think about *Gone with the Wind* again. Margaret Mitchell's descriptions of the burning of Atlanta were nothing short of superb – but do you remember any of them in detail? I guarantee that what you remember most are two wonderful pieces of dialogue from Scarlett and Rhett respectively. Their actual sentences were very short, but in the context of the novel what they said was very powerful and emotive, and said a lot about their characters.

'I'll think about it tomorrow.'
'Frankly, my dear, I don't give a damn.'

In other words, let your characters do the talking. Let them take the credit for showing up their own failings, inadequacies or virtues, or damning themselves quite magnificently.

Example

> Helen knew the woman had seen her, so she had no option but to cross the road, and force a smile to her lips.
>
> 'Beryl, I haven't seen you for ages. I keep meaning to get in touch, but there never seem to be enough hours in the day, what with my job at the estate agent's office and the new flat. How have you been?'
>
> 'Oh, we've been muddling along the same as usual. My Bert had a hernia operation last May, and I'm due to go in for my veins next month. Our daughter Sue had a baby in the summer. Poor little mite suffers from asthma, but the doctor hopes she'll grow out of it. And their Tommy broke his arm recently – '
>
> 'I'm sorry – '
>
> 'Yes, well, it's only to be expected, the way he tears around on that bike of his. He was due to come a cropper one of these days. I don't suppose you heard about old Mr Simmons dropping down dead? I keep telling my Bert he ought to lose some weight, or he'll be next.'

No guesses as to why Helen hasn't been too bothered about keeping in touch with Beryl, whose whole life seems to revolve around illness, and whose conversation consists of little else. You sense that Helen is longing to get away from this dismal woman, who won't let her get a word in edgeways once she's launched into her tirade.

There's a lot of mileage in this piece of dialogue. You learn a great deal about the two characters conversing, but you have also been given brief details of a whole family, which may or not be fleshed out later. When Sue or Bert or Tommy eventually turn up in the story, you already know something about them, because of the way gossipy Beryl bombarded Helen with their doings.

Of course the author could have stated all this in a single paragraph. The author who is apprehensive of writing dialogue would probably have done so, and the passage would have read adequately enough. But the reader wouldn't have known Beryl so well, or sensed Helen's backing away from her. She wouldn't have sympathised with Helen for having to listen to it all, or felt a different kind of sympathy – or impatience – for Beryl and her doom-laden family.

Whatever reaction a reader got from this small interchange, it would be because she was 'hearing' the characters. There's no better way for author and reader to really get under the characters' skins than to let them do the talking.

Chapter 2

PRIMARY PURPOSES OF DIALOGUE

It's generally accepted that the average reader, if there is such a thing, reads a novel for pleasure and entertainment. But there are other reasons. People read books for sheer escapism, to relieve boredom or loneliness, or possibly as an alternative to viewing television. The one thing on which they will all agree is that to 'lose oneself' in the pages of a book is an enjoyable occupation. If they didn't think so, they wouldn't be readers.

They will expect a good story, with interesting characters and, depending on their choice of genre, they will expect a hint (or maybe far more) of romance, mystery, suspense or drama. For the duration of that story, they will wish to be transported into another world that the author has created, and by the end of it, they will want to feel that they knew those characters. They will have identified with them, laughed, cried and swore with them. They will have suffered their anxieties and gloried in their triumphs.

And they will have been involved in their conversations . . .

Just as you, the author, should listen to your characters' voices, and hear what they say as you write their dialogue, don't forget that the reader too, will be giving each of your characters an individual voice. If you have been describing someone well known, perhaps in the media or a member of the royal family, then your reader will know exactly how that person speaks.

But for your fictional characters, the voice as interpreted by your reader cannot possibly be exactly the same one as

15

you imagined it. Don't be alarmed by this statement. Each of your characters has been created by you alone, and only you can really 'hear' it in that form. Therefore the voice that your reader mentally bestows on the character can also only be in his or her own head. It's as if he or she is 'listening' to an acquaintance speaking.

But if you have done your characterisation well, and the words that you put into your characters' mouths are totally compatible with their personalties, then you and your reader should reach a reasonably similar interpretation of your characters' voices.

When readers come to the lines of dialogue in your book, they will mentally say them in their heads too. It may be a completely subconscious thing to do, and maybe you have never considered that point, or paused to realise that you do the same thing when you read a novel. But as long as he or she is satisfied with the characters and their story, the average reader doesn't need to bother with all this analysing of what makes good dialogue. As an author, you do.

Most readers, even if they've never really thought about it before, will agree that when they read a novel about Irish characters, for instance, they automatically read the dialogue with an Irish intonation in their heads. Doing so helps to bring those characters far more readily to life and, if the author has defined them well, especially through their dialogue, it's a very easy and natural thing to do.

Example

> 'Sure and I never meant to hurt you, me darlin'.
> 'Twas the screws in me legs that got me so all-fired
> crochety.'

Well, is that an Irishman speaking, or a Dutchman? It has little more than the flavour of the national tone, but I find it impossible to read such a sentence without hearing the Irish accent in my own head as I read the words. More specific discussion about local accents and regional attributes will come in a later chapter.

But how much more emotive are those two previous sentences of dialogue than by the author putting it all into prose, thus:

> Paddy Murphy was crochety that morning. The screws in his legs were playing him up, and he was extra sharp with his wife over breakfast.

The paragraph gives exactly the same information, but we don't sense the way Paddy is moaning over his poor old legs, and wheedling his wife to forgive him. . . .

GIVING INFORMATION

It's important to think about the primary purposes of dialogue. Novels do not contain dialogue merely to break up the pages of solid prose and narration. Having said that, it is certainly far more pleasing to the eye to have the pages interspersed with both prose and dialogue. But the words you let your characters speak should always be meaningful, and new writers are often guilty of putting trite bits of dialogue into their characters' mouths, simply because they do not appreciate the worth of good dialogue. The end result is merely padding to fill the required pages.

They waste all the wonderful words and telling phrases at their disposal by writing a series of small exchanges that many readers will gloss over. Instead of all this trivial chitchat, they should be imparting that most useful of reasons for letting their characters speak – giving information.

If you supply all the information you need to in a story by writing it all down in prose, you might just as well be writing an essay. A novel needs more than flat prose to make it live. Your characters deserve more than that, and so do your readers. A short story in particular, where every word must count, can be sharpened considerably by the use of informative dialogue.

When you want to include details of some historical event in a story, it's far better to have your characters telling each other about it than to state it all in a block of endless prose that shrieks of all the research notes that you have taken. By letting the characters speak, they, and you, will be informing the readers about your historical event in a painless and non-lecturing way.

It certainly spoils the illusion of the story if a reader becomes aware that he's being educated by some superior author who's checked all the facts, and can't bear to waste a single one of them. It's far more professional, and smoother, to involve your characters in those recorded happenings, in words and actions.

I can't deny that it's very tempting to include all the research that you do, but you need to be wary on this point. For instance, supposing you were writing a Second World War novel set in the time when the dreaded doodlebug (for its time, a sophisticated type of German bomb) made its appearance in warfare. Since the newspapers and wireless bulletins would be full of this news, you could hardly ignore the fact that doodlebugs were falling on London. But you may need to be selective in how much of this information is relevant to the characters in your particular story. Don't be tempted to fill several pages with all the background detail you've discovered about those evil weapons, just for the sake of it.

If your particular novel was set in the wilds of Wales, the advent of the doodlebugs may not be important to your story except as a passing reference. Your characters may not be personally involved at all. But supposing your story was about an evacuee, visited in his Welsh foster home by an older relative who had arrived with bad news. Then you have the ideal opportunity to describe it all in detail to an inquisitive young audience, even though the main part of your story takes place well away from the scene of warfare.

Example

> 'But what was it *like*, Auntie Vi? Did the house come crashing all around you?' Tommy said eagerly, his eyes round with excitement at the thought of such an adventure.

Vi shuddered. 'Don't be daft, young Tommy. A few roof slates fell, that's all,' she lied. 'And don't go asking me too much about those doodlebugs. Nasty, wicked things they are, giving you no warning except for that awful whistling sound, and then nothing. Mind you, the silence just before they hit their targets is worse than all the rest. That's when you know the bomb's got your name on it.'

She hadn't meant to say so much, but somehow the words just kept coming. And she might have known it wouldn't be enough to satisfy the boy.

'Did my bedroom get bombed then? I don't care if it did. Ma said I could sleep in the back room when I go home.'

'You'll be sleeping nowhere in that house, my duck, 'cause it ain't there no more.'

Tommy stared at her. 'Why not? Did the Germans aim straight for our house, then? And where's me Ma? Why didn't she come with you?'

You hardly need telling that his Ma disappeared with the house, and that a lot of trouble looms ahead for Tommy. A few sentences of telling conversation can reveal all the facts that are needed at this stage. The readers have learned a bit about the mechanics of the doodlebugs at the same time, but not so much that they feel they're being 'educated'.

The following extract is from *Scarlet Rebel* (Jean Saunders, Ballantine and Severn House), and is the scene where Charles Stuart arrives on Scottish soil for the first time. There is a relatively small amount of dialogue, but far less prose, and it sets the scene in far fewer and more emotive words than by the author's narration.

'We shall land at a spot a little way from Glenfinnan, sir,' said the man at his elbow.

The prince nodded his agreement. 'It seems abysmally silent,' Charles observed. 'Where are the crowds, the clansmen, the cheering? Do they not know the importance of this day?'

'I am certain that they do, sir. Be patient, I implore ye.'

'Patient I am not,' Charles said shortly.

'We have some way to go yet, sir, and the day is still early. The Highlands are vast, and some will take considerable time to get here. The bishop of Morar will be at the landing place to greet ye, I'm assured of that.'

And a little later:

The bishop bowed low and greeted the prince warmly.

'Welcome, sir. If you will do me the honour to follow me, there is a place where you can rest until the clansmen come.'

'They do not do me the honour of awaiting *me*?' Charles could not resist saying.

'Some are encamped in the hills, sir, but the morning is cold and your time of arrival uncertain.'

'It has taken more than a cold wind to keep me from my people," he retorted, with a small show of arrogance. 'But no matter. Lead the way, my lord bishop.'

A great deal of information is imparted in those two short scenes, and the majority of it is in dialogue. It makes the telling far smoother than if the whole thing was done in a single paragraph of researched facts. Compare it with the following prose narrative of the same events:

Charles Stuart's boat was due to land at a spot a little way from Glenfinnan. There were no welcoming crowds in evidence, and he felt anger mixed with disappointment and his usual impatience. He had not come so far to be ignored by his people. They should surely have been aware of the importance of this day, when their rightful king had returned to them.

This is an adequate enough paragraph, and gives all the information required. But it fails to arouse any emotion in the reader, because it does not show the real emotion of the characters. You can *say* that a character is angry or upset, but you can *show* it far better through dialogue.

Whenever you research historical data, you will always come across many fascinating facts that you will want to incorporate into your novel. And it's very tempting to set them all down and air your knowledge. Sometimes this is a perfectly good way to do it, especially when you want to cover an event that is not totally relevant to your story but which needs to be mentioned in passing and covered quite quickly. But always take a second look at your prose to see if it couldn't be re-told more vividly through dialogue.

When I researched the facts for *Scarlet Rebel*, there were many instances of true coincidences and plots, some of which deserved more than just narrative re-telling. One of them occurred during the horror of Culloden, and is related in the aftermath of the battle, by a minor character giving the information to the central characters – and also to the readers.

'Ye'll have heard o' the rebel laddie with the great likeness to the prince's looks, Jamie,' Moffat went on. ' 'Twas uncanny to be fighting alongside him and hear him shout in the Gaelic when he resembled the other so much – and even worse when he was slain so near to the two of us – '

'Go on, man,' Jamie said brutally, seeing Katrina blanch, but needing to hear what this was all about.

'We heard his call as he lay dying, and plenty redcoats heard it too, Mackinnon. Our man declared that the redcoats had killed their prince. The words threw them all into confusion. Wi' a price on the Stuart's head of thirty thousand pounds, they needed to be sure it was the Stuart who was slain.'

And a little later:

'The redcoats cut off the man's head and have sent it to London for identifying. Until they can be sure the dead man is Charles Stuart, the search for him is slowed down a mite.'

According to the many research sources I consulted for that book, the information described in that dialogue is historically correct. The horror of such an event can be conveyed far more acutely by letting one of the characters relate it, and by having someone else react to it.

You will almost certainly have heard the advice 'show, don't tell' when it comes to writing fiction. In the case of dialogue, I think this should be amended and expanded to 'show through telling' – and always let your characters do the telling where you can.

MOVING THE STORY FORWARD

Another important aspect of using dialogue in fiction is that of moving the story forward. No story can or should remain static, and how to make the transition of time and space is often a source of worry to new writers.

It's an indisputable fact that since the advent of television, even more than in films, we have all become indoctrinated into accepting fast-moving plots and plenty of scene changes. All of these things help to move the story forward and keep the viewer watching. In the same way, moving the story forward at a pace to suit the plot will keep the readers reading.

One of the simplest ways to deal with this movement of time or space is to have your characters contemplating future events by discussing it together. This can be particularly useful when it comes at the end of a chapter. The next chapter can then begin quite naturally and smoothly with the new date or location.

Your readers will be quite happy (and probably relieved) to overlook the fact that you haven't mentioned every single happening between, say, January and April, because you will have already prepared the way for them to know that the story is about to move on. Detailing every single day and every little domestic happening is a sure sign of the amateur, and can make very tedious reading. It also holds up the pace of your novel and slows it down.

Such a transition from one chapter to the next could be applied as follows:

Example
The following would come, say, at the end of Chapter 1:

> 'So when are you actually taking up the new appointment, Mannering?' Carson asked.
> 'The ninth of April is the date that's been finally decided.'
> 'They're giving you just over three months to get your personal effects in order, then,' the other said. 'I suppose it's not a bad way to begin a new year, with the prospect of a new challenge ahead.'
> (Chapter 1 would end there)

The following would be the beginning of Chapter 2:

> 'How do you think you'll like it here, Mannering?' the director of operations said. 'You've come to us at a good time. Spring is particularly fine in this part of the country.'
> (Chapter 2 would then continue)

There's no break in continuity between the ending of Chapter 1 and the beginning of Chapter 2, despite the three months that separate them. Obviously, there would have been far

23

more information about the new job in Chapter 1 before the author reached this concluding scene, but the dialogue effectively bridges the time transition.

The reader is already anticipating Mannering's new job and the challenge that awaits him, and is ready for the story to move forward to the next stage. He has no difficulty in taking in the fact that the ending of the previous chapter took place in January and that, with the beginning of Chapter 2, it's now April.

There was also a smooth location transition in the last example, even though the main piece of information was intended to span the three months between scenes. Dialogue is very effective in bridging locations, whether you are merely moving your characters by car to a picnic, or transporting them between continents or to other worlds, and it needn't always occur at the junction of two chapters.

Example

> 'I have a horrible feeling I'm not going to like the country one bit,' Jill said.
>
> 'You'll change your mind once you get there,' the car driver said.
>
> 'I doubt that. Once a city girl, always a city girl,' she said feelingly. 'All that mud and the prospect of waking up to animal smells and birdsong every morning isn't exactly my scene. And incidentally, why don't you slow down a bit? Seeing all these fields speeding by on these rotten bumpy roads is doing unspeakable things to my insides.'
>
> 'You shouldn't have had bacon and eggs for breakfast then,' he said without sympathy. 'Though you'll be getting plenty of them at the farm, I daresay.'

Plenty of characterisation comes through in those few exchanges, and at the same time the reader is being transported along those bumpy roads with the characters. Depending on

24

what's gone before, she'll be either sympathising or laughing at the way city girl Jill is reacting to the prospect of life on the farm.

REVEALING PRESENT MOOD/EMOTIONAL STATE OF CHARACTERS

This heading really underlines all that has gone before. All the words that you put into your characters' mouths should be revealing more about their personalities. Fictional dialogue is not the same as real-life dialogue, but the author's aim is to make it appear to be real. Fictional dialogue should be as carefully constructed as the most intricate of plots.

To the new writer, this may be somewhat off-putting, especially when you want to get on with your story, and the ideas are white hot in your mind. The last thing you want to do at such a time is to stop and pause over every line of dialogue as if it's some delicate plant that has to be carefully cultivated.

The skill in writing good dialogue can be inborn, and we would all love to be known as natural storytellers. But the techniques can also be learned. If you are the kind of writer who has no difficulty in getting emotions down on paper, and who finds writing dialogue easy, then you are fortunate. The majority of writers, when they begin to write fiction, are far more inhibited.

They worry about what the neighbours might think if they write a steamy love scene, and even more what Great Aunt Mary might say. They worry that the man along the road will give them a nudge-nudge, wink-wink as the review of their suddenly successful blockbuster reveals that the author has insights into shady underworlds he never dreamed she could possibly know about.

That nice little woman he had hardly noticed before, except at his wife's occasional coffee mornings, may be suddenly revealed as someone writing about nineteenth-century brothels or drug barons or the mechanics of murder. But make no mistake about it. If she doesn't write about such things with authority, using the dialogue that such characters would use in the imaginary worlds she has created, then the book will never be published at all.

All inhibitions need to be put aside when you write fiction. It's part of the price you pay. And after all, it's only words on paper. You aren't selling your soul to the devil, even if you write the steamiest romance or the most vicious novel about the Mafia and the underworld. But when all else fails, and you feel you simply *can't* put those awful words into your villain's mouth and still show your face at the supermarket, remember that you can always resort to using a pseudonym on the jacket of your book. Many authors do, for all sorts of reasons.

It's sound advice to construct your sentences of dialogue carefully and make them work for your story and your characters. There's also a strong case for just getting those words down on paper while the scene of dialogue is vivid in your head, and then tidying it up later.

I'm a great believer in writing the chapter of your novel or your short story as quickly as possible, and then revising it as much as is necessary. Don't overdo it. I don't advocate doing so much revision that you take the life and soul out of your writing. But dialogue is one area where revision is often vital. It may involve little more than changing phrases around, or starting a sentence or a piece of dialogue at a different point, in order to get the best meaning out of it.

Revealing your character's present mood or emotional state is often a crucial part of a story. How can you really believe in a character enduring a crisis if you don't hear her speak? You need to wring the withers of your readers, to use a cliché that explains it all so admirably that I see no point in not using it. Though since the withers are the ridge between a horse's shoulder-blades, I'm not too sure how they came to be so succinct in this context. No doubt somebody will tell me.

A character's present mood and emotional state can be summed up in very few actual words of dialogue. The following examples are taken out of context, and without elaboration, but the interpretations convey a possible meaning.

26

Examples

'I'm shattered.'

Interpretation:
He's very tired after a hard day's work.

'Give me a drink, for God's sake.'

Interpretation:
He's just had a terrible shock and is reaching for the first thing to hand to calm him down. Or he's an habitual drinker.

'Get the hell out of here, you bitch.'

Interpretation:
He's just discovered his wife's affair, and is turning her out of the house.

'I just can't face another day without him.'

Interpretation:
She is confiding in a friend after the death of her husband. Or her young son has been kidnapped.

In all of those brief sentences of dialogue, the reader is emotionally involved with the characters' feelings. The same explanations could be given just as easily in the prose, as shown in the possible interpretations, but the reader would be far less interested in how the character was feeling. Once those emotions are touched and aroused, then you've got your reader hooked.

REVEALING PRIOR EVENTS AND FUTURE HOPES

Example

'Did the casting director say anything to you about next month's rehearsals?' John said.

Angela nodded. 'I don't hold out much hope for me though. Of course I'd love the part of Ophelia, but I was so hopeless in *Pygmalion*, I doubt if he'll want to use me for anything but an extra next time.'

'You were a little lacking in the Cockney accent, perhaps, but it wasn't as if you were playing Eliza – '

'You don't have to remind me,' she said, and then she brightened. 'At least I'm under contract for the Christmas pantomime. I've always wanted to play Principal Boy.'

It didn't need a whole chapter of a novel to lead you into the situation here. Angela's acting wasn't too good as the flower seller in *Pygmalion*, which was the theatre company's last production. She doesn't hold out much hope for a starring role in the next one. But since she's an optimist, she's looking ahead to Christmas. She's going to be in panto, and she's all set to be Principal Boy. And the reader knows what was past, present, and what's going to happen in the future, because John and Angela have just told him so.

Chapter 3

AND THERE'S MORE ...

Not all the characters in a novel can be the most brilliant conversationalists. You will sometimes create those who habitually make mundane comments, because that is part of their personality, but even those mundane comments will have a purpose. They will be part of such a character's make-up. The character who always talks in clichés, for instance, or who is long-winded and pedantic, has his place in a story, especially if he is there to show up the sparkling wit of the others by contrast.

It's always a good idea to create contrasting characters who can bounce off one another, but beware that you don't caricature the kind of stereotypes that often seem to go together.

The dumb/slower-on-the-uptake sidekick can always be a foil for the cleverness of his chief detective, whether or not they are in the regular police force or just amateur sleuths. But how many Captain Hastings and Hercule Poirot/Doctor Watson and Sherlock Holmes combinations can the world take?

There are more modern equivalents of such pairings, and there's no doubting their usefulness, whose effectiveness is shown to best advantage through dialogue. Unfortunately, if it's not done well you run the risk of merely portraying the pompous know-all and the sycophantic hanger-on.

Nevertheless, even the cleverest detective must have someone with whom to discuss his case, or else the reader will

29

never know what goes on in his brilliant mind. Every main character in a novel needs a confidante, and by the very nature of the word, this is a person in whom he will confide all the information that we, the readers, need to know.

In a family saga, especially one involving a family power struggle, the characters must necessarily be portrayed very differently, or they would all be clones of each other. No two family members are exactly alike, and sibling rivalry is an especially good area in which to create good and contrasting characters.

Their backgrounds will be similar, but they may have differing opinions on people and places, music, books and so on. And unless they have been estranged from each other, either through circumstance or design, they will talk to each other. It would be a pretty strange family if they didn't.

CREATING ATMOSPHERE
Dialogue can be at its most useful when creating atmosphere. By bringing all the senses into play, you involve your readers in the action very quickly. Letting your characters describe what they see and hear and feel, by relating it to someone else, can bring a scene vividly to life, whether it's romantic or macabre or frightening. You can also use description of a place to great effect by letting one character tell another of her experiences.

Such atmospheric scenes can be almost all dialogue with very little prose to interrupt the flow, as long as the two characters are clearly defined. This is also something to be used with care, as it can produce a ping-pong look to the page. In Example 1 the ping-pong effect of such dialogue is avoided by the differing lengths of the 'speeches'.

    1 'Tell me what you see,' Doctor Denby said gently.

    Although Ellie's eyes were open, somehow she was no longer on the psychiatrist's couch, but somewhere in her past.

    'I see – I see a big old house with ivy growing

over its walls. Inside the house there are a great many rooms and they all have tall windows. Lots of windows.'

'Look through the windows, Ellie.'

She began to breathe more rapidly. 'I can see – oh, yes. There's a narrow curving bay just beyond the house, and it's surrounded by cliffs. I can't see them properly, but I know they're there, jutting out into the sea, like jagged knives. They frighten me.'

'What do you hear?'

After a pause, she shuddered. 'I can hear the sea. It's pounding against the cliffs like – like an endless drumming, but there's a different sound too. It's like splintering wood. A boat, perhaps. Is it a boat?'

'I don't know. You tell me.'

'Yes. It's a boat. Oh God – it's breaking up against the cliffs, and everyone is drowned.'

'Everyone?'

'Yes – no, not everyone. I'm not drowned. I'm saved. I'm taken to the big house with the tall windows, but I don't know where I am any more. I can't remember – '

In this example Ellie was 'seeing' and 'hearing' a past event that had a profound effect on her life. The Cornish (or Welsh or Yorkshire or Scottish) coastline and gothic atmosphere were being evoked as they were being drawn unwillingly out of her subconscious. She was reliving some terrible event in her life under hypnosis, but it needed the dialogue to reveal the full extent of her past.

2   'I hate graveyards,' Harry muttered. 'Why did we have to come here when there's not even a bit of moonlight to see a hand in front of our faces?'

'Stop your griping. We're well hidden by this fog, and there's only us and the spooks, and they ain't talking,' Reg leered, and then clutched Harry's arm. 'Bloody hell, what's that over there behind that headstone?'

'Shut up, Reg,' Harry snapped. 'I knew this was a daft idea, and my feet are wet through already. There's nobody meeting us tonight, and if there is, I ain't waiting for 'em.'

A sudden moaning sound curdled his blood for a moment. Then he heard Reg's laugh, and lashed out at him.

'You damn fool. Do you want to let the whole world know we're here on the loose?'

In this example the characters' and readers' imaginations were aroused by the blatant fear put into one character's head by the other. The scene is plain enough, and is emphasised by the choice of words used: 'dark graveyard'; 'spooks'; 'fog'; 'wet feet'; 'moaning'; 'curdled his blood'. There is also a sixth-sense element brought in here. The reader almost expects something ghoulish to happen, and may or may not get it.

3 'What do you remember most about New York, Sal?'

Her eyes were dreamy. 'I could say everything, but if I had to cut it down to the most vivid memories, I'd say Central Park first, which was like a great green oasis in the middle of the city where we went roller-skating on Sunday mornings.'

'Did you like the skyscrapers?'

'Oh yes, of course! Some of them were like huge glass and concrete mountains reaching up to the sky and shutting out the light, and the view from the Empire State Building took your breath away. Did you know that when you've been whisked up to the top on the fastest elevator imaginable, you can feel the building sway?'

Alice shuddered. 'No, I didn't know that,

thanks. So tell me about the Statue of Liberty. Did it come up to all your expectations?'

Sal smiled. 'I'll say it did. And the best sight of all was when the plane came into land at night, and we saw the statue floodlit, like a little green ghost in the ocean.'

'*Green?*'

Sal sighed. 'Don't you know anything, Alice? She's made out of copper, and when she's floodlit she glows green.'

You may argue that Example 3 is more informative than atmospheric, but the resulting dialogue also allows Alice to share Sal's sights and experiences. If it makes the reader curious and interested about New York, then it has succeeded. In the last sentence, when Sal refers to the statue as *she*, an element of familiarity and affection is brought in. This is a far more subtle way of describing what most people know about the statue than by referring to her as Miss Liberty.

A descriptive dialogue scene should always appeal to the senses where possible, rather than by stating the basic geographical facts. Sal is 'feeling' the sway from the top of the Empire State Building. When Alice shuddered, you sensed that she was 'feeling' it too. Sal was 'seeing' again the evocative green glow of the Statue of Liberty at night. Despite her having always wanted to visit it, it's the more unusual personal memory that sticks most vividly in her mind, and makes the event seem more real to the reader.

Whenever you want to create atmosphere through dialogue, try to employ as many of the senses as you can. By allowing all these vicarious experiences to be shown through an exchange of words, the scenes are brought more vividly to life for the reader than by merely stating facts from a reference book.

You could, of course, glean all the above facts from a reference book without ever going to New York. The trick is to persuade your readers to believe that your characters, through their authoritative dialogue, know the place well.

SHOWING ATTITUDES AND CONFLICTS

No two characters in your story are going to be exactly alike, and nor should they be. Each should be unique, with the ability to express themselves in their own way. If you fail to give each one this ability, you're missing out on a vital fictional skill. Each character will have thoughts and feelings and opinions, and while some will be articulate and academic, others may be ill-educated and unable to say all that they feel.

Your job is to convey all that cleverness of speech as well as the frustration at not being able to convey the right words. It's sometimes far easier to do the first. But whatever kind of character you have created, you need to put yourself into his shoes and, more importantly, to speak his words in your head. Conflict is your greatest asset in creating good dialogue. Without conflict in a novel your writing will be bland at best and boring at worst.

Fitting your characters' words to their role in life is one of the basic requirements in showing their attitudes. Would a wealthy politician, brought up in a life of luxury, have the same attitude towards going abroad as a boy from the slums? He certainly would not, and in a novel that involved one or other of those characters going to Italy or France or wherever you chose to send them, those attitudes would come through in their dialogue.

Inventing characters with contrasting lifestyles is a marvellous way of opening up all these traits. You need no more than a smattering of dialogue to distinguish different attitudes and life-styles, as in the following examples.

1 'I do beg your pardon –' Sir Angus Philpott-Gore's apology died abruptly, as he saw the unwashed youth who had brushed against him in the crowded airport.

' 'S all right, chief, I ain't hurt, just looking for me mates. Bit of a crush 'ere, ain't it?'

'Excuse me,' Sir Angus said, moving quickly away.

2 'I've always voted Labour, and no damn kid of mine is going to tell me different, so don't start on with your poncey ideas. When you can argue that black's white, I might be convinced, but that'll be a long time coming, my son.'

'You're being pig-headed, Dad – '

'And you needn't think that a university education gives you the right to come back home and tell me what's what!' Al shouted. 'You and your bloody debates aren't going to change a damn thing. Is that all I pay these fees for, so that you can swan around and think you can change the world? When I was your age I'd knuckled down and – '

'Oh God, don't start on that again. And don't go on about paying my fees. I won a scholarship, remember?'

'I'm still bloody keeping you, aren't I? You should be out earning by now, same as any self-respecting kid. And keep a civil tongue in your head when you speak to me.'

'There's no point, is there? You never listen.'

BUILDING UP CHARACTER SUSPENSE

To keep the reader's interest in your plot and characters, you need to keep your story moving forward. Too much introspection always slows it down, so any flashbacks that you use are most effective when filtered in in small doses rather than in large passages. This is most smoothly done through dialogue.

A character who is worried about something happening in the future, or in dread of past misdemeanours or old secrets haunting him, is an interesting character. By showing those fears and anxieties you double the interest your reader shows in him. A character with a secret to hide is also a character worth writing about. Many of the examples already shown in this chapter will demonstrate these points.

35

In my novel *The Bannister Girls* (Jean Saunders, Grafton)
Sir Fred Bannister has a secret that has just been discovered
by his favourite daughter, Angel. She's devastated by the discovery, and doesn't know what to do about it. She hates the
fact that she now shares the secret. Finally she's compelled
into confiding in her best friend.

'He has a mistress. Doesn't that shock you? My so-
respectable father!'

Margot knew what it must have cost Angel to
confess to something that wasn't her fault, but
which nonetheless touched every one of her family.
And it wasn't so staggering, since Margot had already guessed the truth.

'No, it doesn't shock me,' she said evenly. 'Your
father's human, like all of us. The Royals have had
mistresses and lovers for centuries. Why should we
lesser ones be so different?'

'I don't care about Royals! I only care about *us*!'

'Isn't that being a little selfish?'

Angel turned to look at her now, her face
flushed with anger. To her friend, it was a healthier
emotion than the blank bewilderment that had
masked her face for much of the time since arriving
on Margot's doorstep.

'*Selfish?* It's my father who's being selfish – '

'Who's he hurting? Not your mother, who's always been so self-sufficient she probably only ever
needed him for procreation, and once all that sor-
did business was done with, I'll bet she never
allowed him into her bedroom again. Can you
deny it? Remember how wicked we used to feel at
college, taking bets on it?'

'I know, but – '

'He's certainly not hurting Louise, who by all
accounts is well rid of that chinless wonder, Stan-
ley, and good luck to her with her haggis man.
Ellen couldn't care less what your father does, as

long as she goes her own sweet way. So that leaves you – Daddy's darling. Face it, Angel, you're jealous.'

Angel glared at her.

'Don't be ridiculous – '

'You're just plain, old-fashioned jealous. You can't bear to think that some other woman has claimed your father's affections. All these years when your dear Mama has been frigid and unloving, he's lavished all that generous love on little Angel, and now he's found a real warm flesh-and-blood woman. At least, I presume that's what she is. Do you care so little for him that you begrudge him that?'

SUSTAINING READER INTEREST AND CURIOSITY

Keeping up your reader's curiosity depends largely on the twists and turns of your plot. Writing a detailed synopsis before you begin your short story or novel will keep you on the right track as to pace and balance. A synopsis may be very detailed, or no more than a rough plan to show you where your story is going, but it's a useful guide to keep by you as you're writing.

It will also indicate in your story where nothing much is happening and where you may want to pep up a scene with some bridging dialogue. A synopsis usually resembles an essay, and you may find it useful to mark the passages where big scenes of dialogue can be especially valid. At all the key points of your plot where the action changes, or time moves on, you can effectively dangle a hook for the reader by letting your characters talk through the transition.

Always aim to keep your reader curious. If she can see from the beginning of your story exactly what's going to happen, she may not bother to read any more. This really underlines the value of the synopsis rather than blundering on through a story without knowing where you're going with it. You can work out in advance the twists and turns that are going to take the reader by surprise and keep her reading. You can further this curiosity even more by giving her a sense of anticipation:

> 'Aunt Meg's coming to stay for a month,' Amy announced.
>
> 'Oh no! I can't stand the old trout for a week, let alone a month!' Lilian wailed.
>
> Amy folded up the letter without showing it to her sister. 'I don't know what you've got against her. She was always sweet to us when we were kids, and I like her, even if she is a bit eccentric.'
>
> 'You can say that again,' Lilian said feelingly. 'She's more like an old witch, if you ask me.'
>
> 'Well, nobody did.'

No prizes for guessing that there's sure to be trouble when Aunt Meg arrives on the scene. The very mention of her name has stirred up old childhood memories in each of the two sisters, and it's easy to see which one was the favourite with Aunt Meg. The word 'eccentric' and Lilian's remark that Aunt Meg was 'more like an old witch' could give you a strong clue as to the kind of story this is going to be. I'd love to know just how Aunt Meg is going to turn the lives of these two girls upside down. I'd be curious . . .

SUMMARISING PLOT MOVEMENTS
It's such a simple, yet completely effective device, to summarise your plot movements through the characters' dialogue, yet it's something that many writers ignore. Plot movements can be interpreted as being those that have already happened, or those that are to come. By a quick resumé of either by the characters, the reader can be swiftly carried along in the story.

As an example for a romantic novel, imagine that two friends are in a state of indecision about whether or not to take temporary jobs abroad. The younger they are the greater will be the conflict you will have already established between them and parents and/or friends and colleagues. Making them female will increase any such conflict, since females are generally supposed to be more at risk abroad.

Imagine that they are just eighteen years old. The reader will already be wondering whether or not these two girls actually do go abroad or chicken out under pressure or self-doubt, and most readers will be willing them on to go. Since this is a romantic novel, it's probably essential that they do go, or there's no story. From the brief scenario given above you could already be constructing some kind of dialogue in your mind. It will inevitably involve some conflict or argument, either with each other or with other people.

Such conflict could go on at length, and probably has done so already in this story, but there may well come a point when it's useful to sum everything up neatly. The dialogue to summarise the plot movements so far could go like this:

'What have we got to lose, Helen?' Sue was getting impatient now. 'Let's stop all this dithering and check out the fors and againsts, OK? We're both bored with working at Gould's Plastics, we're fed up with all the hassle we're getting at home, we don't have any commitments since you ditched Ed Phillips, *and* we'll be making far more money than we've been doing so far.'

'You can't guarantee that. As for no commitments, I didn't think you'd want to run out on John for the whole summer. Isn't he a consideration any more?'

'I'm not running out on him. But I need some space and this job is the ideal way to get it. He's been getting far too serious lately, and I'm not ready to settle for the telly and slippers routine.'

'All right,' Sue said. 'Those were the fors. Now what about the againsts? We don't have any money to take with us, so if it all goes wrong, we'll be stuck. We don't even know if these job offers are genuine. We don't know anybody in Spain, and we don't speak the language – '

'We could always take a crash course. They do them on cassettes now – '

'And I hate foreign food, it always makes me feel ill – '

Sue lost her temper. 'God, Helen, you're so damn boring, I wonder why I ever asked you to come with me at all!'

'So do I,' Helen grinned. 'So, does that mean we're going or not?'

Well, what do you think? Of course they'll go to Spain, and the outcome is up to the author. But that small scene opens up all kinds of possibilities for future events. Through the brief plot summaries, you can already anticipate the likelihood of Helen falling ill with a stomach bug, misunderstandings through language difficulties, and sudden nostalgia for the old boyfriends.

Sue can finally realise that John is/is not for her. Family problems can occur, sending one or the other of them back to England and leaving the other one to fend alone. Sue is clearly the stronger character, and therefore the book's natural heroine, for want of a better word.

This kind of plot summary through dialogue can be used to great effect in a novel involving battle movements. It's a common device used in films, when the commander has his troops all gathered together, and is pointing out all the battle events so far by means of a pointer on a wall map. It's a tried and tested method of telling the troops, and it also tells the rest of us.

In print, it's perfectly acceptable to summarise these things in a single paragraph of prose, as I have often done, bringing in the character's involvement at the very end of the paragraph. The alternative is to have one character telling another about the disastrous events that led them up to the present time.

It all depends on whether or not you want to bring the

scene sharply into focus through the dialogue, or if the information conveyed is to be a mere transition in time. Neither is wrong, and the choice depends on the pace of your plot, and how the events depicted affect your characters.

If you were describing D-Day and none of your characters was physically involved in it, you may just want to detail it as a passage of time before your characters took up their own story again. A serious, male-orientated wartime novel set at that precise time would hardly ignore such a major event.

But supposing you were writing a different kind of novel, with younger characters? Maybe your juvenile characters have launched their father's own past-its-prime fishing boat because they were caught up with the excitement of the day, and saw this as a bit of a lark in getting to France. Then you would have a very different scenario, and the adventure and excitement and drama of it all would be shown to best effect through their own dialogue:

> 'The bloody boat's leaking,' Jim suddenly yelled out in a fright. He grabbed one of his father's old fishing pails and began furiously baling out.
>
> 'It's all right,' Brian shouted back above the splutter of the engine. 'Dad said there was a bit of a leak, but it'll plim up as soon as we're under way.'
>
> 'We are under bloody way. We're halfway to France!'
>
> Brian's laugh was uneasy. 'We ain't nothing like halfway yet, bruth. And I can't see nothing through this spray. Have you got the compass?'
>
> 'I thought you had it.'
>
> 'Well, that's just wonderful,' Brian snapped. 'Now we don't know if we're on course or not.'
>
> 'Why don't we know?'
>
> 'Because this ain't the north circular, dummy. They don't put road markings on the English Channel.'
>
> Jim peered through the gloom of early morning.

41

'Where are all the rest of the boats then?' he said hoarsely.

You can see disaster looming all the way from this small scene. Two young boys are *en route* to German-occupied France with totally inadequate equipment in a leaking fishing boat that obviously belongs to their father. Whatever the outcome, the loss of the boat is going to cause ructions at home, the anticipation of which will add to the boys' anxieties and conflicts.

Every author would have a different idea of how this dialogue scene and consequent story could be developed. This applies to any of the examples in this book. One of the most useful exercises for a beginning fiction writer is to practise such small scenes without all the trappings of the plot to worry about. Give yourself a couple of characters and a setting and develop their dialogue.

The dialogue you invent may or may not come at the beginning of a story. It doesn't matter. The important thing is to get into the habit of writing in dialogue and not to be afraid of tackling it. It may even trigger you into working out a more detailed character analysis. From there it may not be such a big step to inventing a plot for a short story or a novel, simply because you have got so interested in the characters and their predicament. Great oaks from little acorns do grow . . .

Chapter 4

NOW YOU'RE TALKING

Dialogue? Of course you'll include dialogue in a novel. But however determined you are to try to make your characters talk in a natural and realistic way, you may sometimes get so carried away by the storyline that you find you have written whole pages of prose without any dialogue at all.

Don't be too dismayed if this happens to you. It may not be such a bad thing, because it also means you are being carried along by the enthusiasm of your writing and the motivation of your characters. The point is that you should be prepared to go back over the pages of prose you have written, and see where the scenes can be lifted, expanded and brought more visually to life, by introducing dialogue.

Your characters will converse with one another in all kinds of situations, and many scenes occur in fiction that could be enhanced by such rewriting. Not all of them will benefit in this way, and I don't suggest that you rewrite everything just for the sake of using those inverted commas. But always try to see where the flatness of the prose can be lifted by conversation.

Example

1   The whole platoon crept stealthily through the bushes, pausing to listen every now and then for the slightest sound of branches snapping or leaves

rustling. The situation was taut, strained, and each man had his own gutful of fear, and his own private thoughts of hell in this steaming jungle. The whole idea was to take the enemy by surprise, but the constant feeling of being watched made them certain that they were as much the hunted as the hunters.

2 The whole platoon crept stealthily through the bushes. As the officer raised his hand for silence, the squaddies crouched down, muttering and shifting uncomfortably in the steamy heat of the jungle.

'Christ, I can't stand much more of this,' said one in a low hoarse voice. 'Every time we hear a twig snapping or a leaf rustling, he's sure it's a sniper – '

'Shut up, can't you?' snarled another. 'You're asking to get your head blown off – '

The first man shivered, smelling the rankness of his own sweat and that of his companions. He stank with fear.

'We're caught like rats in a trap, and you bloody well know it as well as I do.'

Either piece of writing describes the situation perfectly well. But in Example 2, even though none of the soldiers is named, the feeling of fear is intensified through the dialogue. We know how *they* feel, and not just the overall view of an imminent jungle confrontation with an unseen enemy.

In that example, I deliberately left all the soldiers unnamed. The officer may well be the central character in a story involving this scene, or it may be one of the men. By naming whichever of them you have chosen as your hero, you would automatically give him more prominence in the scene. If you name your hero, and none of the others, he becomes even more prominent, as in Example 3 of the same scene:

3 The whole platoon crept stealthily through the bushes. As the officer raised his hand for silence, the squaddies crouched down, muttering and shifting uncomfortably in the steamy heat of the jungle.

'Christ, I can't stand much more of this,' Carter said in a low hoarse voice. 'Every time we hear a twig snapping or a leaf rustling, he's sure it's a sniper –'

'Shut up, can't you?' snarled the man next to him. 'You're asking to get your head blown off – '

Carter shivered, smelling the rankness of his own sweat and that of his companions. He stank with fear.

'We're caught like rats in a trap, and you bloody well know it as well as I do.'

WORD ORDER PATTERNS

You can change the entire meaning of a piece of dialogue by means of the correct – or incorrect – word order. You can emphasise the points you want to bring out – or you can submerge them, simply because you have put the words your characters say in the wrong order. Getting it wrong is perilously easy to do. Getting it right is just as easy if you give a little thought to the construction of your own sentences, and say them aloud in the way you want your characters to say them. This is the best way of getting your emphasis right.

Changing word order may also involve using different punctuation to achieve your desired effect. Always remember that none of your sentences is written in stone, and can always be changed.

The emphasis in the following few simple sentences of dialogue can be altered dramatically, depending on the order of the words. No qualifying characters' names or adverbs are given, and the reader's interpretation of the sentences rely simply on the word order.

Example

1 'We're going to the pictures tonight.'
2 'Tonight, we're going to the pictures.'

Example 1 is flatter, has a more complacent sound to it, and is no more than a statement of fact from one character to another. Example 2 gives more importance to the date or the time, and the speaker is more decisive. His tone also implies more dominance over the person he's addressing.

3 'I put the document here somewhere, I'm sure.'
4 'I'm sure I put the document here somewhere.'

Example 3 makes the speaker seem a bit unsure, and doubting his own efficiency, despite his words. You can imagine him searching frantically for the missing document. Example 4 makes him sound more confident. His sureness is emphasised by putting it early in the sentence. The impression is that of a person with everything in neat order, who will soon find what he's looking for. Can't you almost hear him saying next: 'Ah, here it is!'?

Such tiny and almost insignificant changes to strengthen the writing can make all the difference to the way your readers 'hear' your characters speak.

Quite often you will find sentences improve by turning them around completely. In the haste of composing dialogue, our thoughts run away with themselves, and the dialogue can often be improved simply by rewriting the sentence using the same phrases, but in a different order. Sometimes the middle or end of the sentence should really be at the beginning, and it's worth experimenting with sentences to see how to get the most impact and accurate meaning.

Example

1 'When I want your opinion, I'll ask for it, and not before.'

2 'I'll ask for your opinion when I want it, and not before.'
3 'There's nothing to be afraid of in travelling alone to Vienna, I assure you, Madam.'
4 'I assure you, Madam, there's nothing to be afraid of in travelling alone to Vienna.'

There's a subtle difference in tone in each pair of examples, which you should 'hear' in your head. In each set, the second sentence gives the speech more importance because the speaker announces himself first. There are so many ways of writing dialogue, and so many variations of a sentence, and in the end it all depends on the author's preference. But changing the word order of your sentences is one of the simplest ways of seeing if you can sharpen up the impact of your dialogue, and in doing so, define your characters more clearly.

CLIMAX AND BATHOS
The climax in a short story or novel occurs at the end, or near-end, when all the loose ends of the plot are tied up. The murderer is brought to justice; the villain gets his come-uppance; the romantic hero and heroine find true love; the disillusioned wife decides that staying married is better than no marriage at all, etcetera etcetera. Whatever conclusion the story merits is its climax.

A climax within dialogue is achieved in much the same way as all the events in a story or novel. Everything leads up to a final dramatic point, with the character making brief statements in ascending order of importance, leading to the most dramatic one of all.

Examples

1 'You can offer me ten, fifty, a thousand dollars – I wouldn't sell for less than a million.'
2 'If I had to give up my home, my children or my life, I'd still do it.'

Each of these sentences would be part of an explanatory scene and is merely shown to give the idea of using climax within the dialogue. It can be a useful method of allowing a character to speak emotionally, passionately or dramatically, particularly in a tense situation. It can also underline a character's strength, doggedness, determination, recklessness, foolhardiness, bravado or heroism.

Bathos is the virtual opposite to climax, and is a kind of anti-climax. A passage of dialogue involving bathos would begin with a sense of drama or a wish to impress, but would end on an incongruous note. The well-known phrase 'from the sublime to the ridiculous' sums up bathos admirably. It can be very effective in dialogue.

Examples

1 'We visited the Aswan High Dam early in the morning, the Aga Khan's Mausoleum in the afternoon, and the flea market after dinner.'
2 'There was blood everywhere, all over the body, the carving knife, and on Granny's reading glasses.'

In Example 1 you have the grandeur and solemnity of the great architectural wonders of Egypt, and are brought back to earth with the image of the flea market.

In Example 2, the homely mention of Granny's reading glasses, coming at the end of the sentence regarding the more serious matters of the blood, the body, and the carving knife, becomes the incongruous factor. Depending on the story, they could also be emotive or endearing for the reader. Or they could be sinister. After all, was Granny the victim, the witness or the murderer?

EFFECTIVE PAUSES
When we talk to each other in real life, our sentences are often incomplete. We stammer, we hesitate, we repeat ourselves, we apologise, we use the wrong words, we interrupt,

we rush on without thinking, or we stop to deliberate on what to say next.

In fiction, all these things can occur, but to use everything in exactly the way they happen in real life would make a real jumble of dialogue. We have to be selective, and even though we use the dashes, the pauses, the hesitations and so on, they should be as carefully constructed as if we were writing a straight passage of prose.

You may have heard actors – and especially certain stand-up comedians – revealing that all those *ad libs* in their performances were as carefully rehearsed as the rest of the script. *Ad libs* are usually full of meaning, even though they sound like such throwaway lines, and are sometimes highly charged with innuendo. The essence of their success lies in their delivery and their effective pauses, and this technique can be just as successful in fictional dialogue.

The pause is effective for your characters, and for your reader, when you want to push a point home. Your pause can occur by the use of a dash between phrases. It can be brought about by breaking the speech into several parts, either by a qualifying adverb or a piece of prose. A character may pause to draw on his cigar in the middle of speaking. Or he may pause long enough to let his eyes narrow thoughtfully, letting the reader into his calculating mind at that moment.

Note. When you use this method of pausing, it's arguable whether or not you indent too often or at all. It depends on the effect you're trying to create. It's still effectively one piece of speech by one character, however many pauses may occur. If you were writing a Shakespeare soliloquy, you may well want to indent here and there, if only to avoid an entire page of dialogue from one person, but most of us aren't writing in Shakespeare's style. Unless the speech is very long with numerous pauses, it's usual to keep it all within one paragraph.

Examples

1 'I can't think straight any more,' Mary said, trembling. 'My head feels as if it's ready to burst, and

besides – ' she bit her lip in real distress now. 'If you don't loosen these ropes, you're going to cut off my circulation –' she swallowed at the thought – 'and much good any ransom money will do you if I'm dead when they find me.'

There are several pauses in this brief piece of dialogue. They are there to ensure sympathy for the character, Mary, and to increase the feeling of suspense. They also give the reader time to digest what's happening, and to experience what Mary's going through. The use of the dashes indicates a pause while the character is thinking what to say next. The reader will also pause in his reading at this point.

After 'distress now' the sentence ends, beginning the dialogue again with a new sentence, which emphasises its importance. This sentence is completely broken up by Mary's 'she swallowed at the thought' and continues afterwards as though 'she swallowed at the thought' is a stage aside. It's sometimes easier to think of such pauses as simply that.

2   'Why don't you answer me, Greg?' she asked. As she waited for his reply, she imagined everything that could go wrong. He didn't want her after all, the timing was wrong, he hadn't meant all those things he had said about the divorce ... 'Well? Are we going to France or aren't we? You can't expect me to wait for ever.'

In this piece of dialogue the reader is given a summing-up of everything in the narrator's mind. The reader probably already knows much of it from the story so far, but given in this way at a dramatic part of the story, it makes an effective and emotive pause. It makes her – and the character – wonder whether Greg is a rat after all, or if he and the character have a future together. It holds up the action for a while.

This can also be done at far greater length than in a single speech. Holding up the action by interspersing dialogue with prose creates a different kind of effective pausing, but with the same ultimate effect. It keeps your readers from knowing

50

everything at once. Your effective pauses will allow them to use their own senses in order to enhance your characters' dialogue. You could just as easily write Example 2 as follows:

'Why don't you answer me, Greg?' she asked.

As she waited for his reply, she imagined everything that could go wrong. He didn't want her after all, the timing was wrong, he hadn't meant all those things he had said about the divorce . . .

'Well? Are we going to France or aren't we? You can't expect me to wait for ever.'

In the above example, you may choose to break the dialogue into separate paragraphs, because the prose information is longer. Either way, you are holding up the action for the reader, and increasing the anticipation of what's to come.

3 She glimpsed the crushed leg beneath the sodden army blanket, and saw the blood seeping through.

'Tell me what I can do for you, Private.' Even as she said it, she knew there was nothing anyone could do. 'Can I get you a cigarette – or maybe you don't smoke – ' Oh God, what a stupid, stupid thing to say to a dying man! She tried again. 'Can I make you more comfortable? Some tea, perhaps?' Now she sounded pathetic, condescending, as if this was a garden party. 'I'm so sorry. I'm not helping at all, am I?'

She stood up clumsily, and felt him clawing at her arm as he begged her not to go. So she was some use after all.

There's all the pathos and frustration in the world in this short passage, and its effectiveness is mainly due to the pauses between the sentences of dialogue. In this case it would be less effective to break it down into several bitty paragraphs. All the woman's sympathy is contained and conveyed in the one block of writing.

YOUR CHARACTER IS ONLY THINKING

Authors have differing ideas on how to express their characters' thoughts. It seems to bother a great many new authors, and conveying thoughts come halfway between writing dialogue and prose. The great thing is to avoid using inverted commas for characters' thoughts, since this confuses a thought sequence with audible speech. It's smooth, and perfectly adequate, simply to begin a thought sentence as if it's part of the prose, as in the example below, ensuring that you use a separate paragraph for the character's thoughts.

> **1** Why did I ever allow him to come near me? she thought. It's not even as if I liked him very much, and I certainly don't intend to repeat the performance.

You will note that the thoughts are written in the first person, just as if the character was saying them aloud. Assuming that this story was written from the third person viewpoint, you should then use the words 'she thought' between the 'thought' sentences.

When you continued with the story, you would start a new paragraph, keeping the above thought sequence contained. It's not strictly dialogue, but neither is it regular prose and it needs to be well defined. Readers would accept the above method readily, and it wouldn't interrupt the flow of the story.

If you were beginning the paragraph in another way, you might start the thought sentence with a capital letter, as follows:

> **2** She thought, Why did I ever allow him to come near me? It's not even as if I like him very much, and I certainly don't intend to repeat the performance.

Of the two examples, I personally think the first is better, since using the capital letter for the beginning of the actual thought sentences seems a little clumsy to me, and I prefer the use of the pause-phrase 'she thought' in the middle of the sequence. But it's up to you.

Another way in which I have used thought sequences is to use underlining in the text. In the printed version of the book this appears as italics. Some authors use this method as a matter of course, but it can become tedious and rather bitty to read if used too often.

I have found it more effective to use underlining when a thought is to be especially emphasised or show some significance in the story. Or when a sudden thought or memory occurs in the character's mind as in several examples below from *To Love and Honour* (Jean Saunders, Grafton and Severn House). Amy's memories of her Gran's workaday words often come back to her unexpectedly, and occur sharply in her mind.

> **3** *Bugger me*, Amy thought, reverting to Gran's patois when anything befuddled her thinking. *Did I really say all that? Next thing I know, Ronald Derbisham will be throwing me out on my ear, with Bert following . . .*

> **4** *Good God, gel*, Gran Moore's voice seemed to censure her, *what's that imagination o' yours putting you through now?*

And later, at her awful discovery of her own identity:

> **5** Amy gave a dragging breath. *Oh, Tommy, Tommy, why did you leave me? Even if I was never meant to know the truth, I loved you desperately as an uncle. Why couldn't we have gone on the way we were so that I had somebody to lean on . . .?*

OCCUPATIONS AND AGE-GROUPS
It's essential that you let your characters use the correct style

and manners in their dialogue to correspond with their occupations or careers. If you are writing about a character in the newspaper world, his dialogue would be filled with newspaper jargon – not so much that it's indecipherable to readers, but certainly enough to make him sound authoritative.

Every occupation has its own peculiar words and phrases, and one of the perils of writing dialogue about a world you don't know, is getting the language wrong. Some research is essential if you're writing about a lifestyle that's unfamiliar to you.

Television has made such research considerably easier. From upmarket speech to downmarket slang, it's all there for the researching. We can all observe how MPs behave in the House of Commons, for instance, and the forms of address used between them.

Programmes such as *Lovejoy* or *Minder* take us into a very different kind of world. Series such as *Eastenders*, *Coronation Street*, *Brookside*, *Neighbours* and so on give us words and phrases we might never otherwise know. If you can't see such programmes, and need information into different terminology, almost all the 'soaps' have spawned paperback books to accompany them.

It's easy enough to go to a library to find a book on any subject you care to name, and very often you need little more than the flavour of the occupation or career to make it sound authentic in the prose. But as soon as your characters begin to talk about their photographic equipment, their expensive yachts or their day as a theatre nurse, then you had better get the language and the jargon right.

People of different age groups also differ in their style of speaking. A young child speaks far slower than a teenager. As people grow older their speech begins to slow down again, and most elderly people speak more slowly and deliberately than when they were younger.

It's impossible and foolish to try and generalise, but it's a useful guide to keep these things in mind when constructing your characters' dialogue. You may choose to define some of your characters by letting them speak in the opposite way to the norm, which gives them more impact. Your particular old gentleman in your story may speak in the quickfire manner of Field Marshal Viscount Montgomery, and this will be a part of his nature and personality.

Just as you pay attention to the lifestyles and occupations of your characters in terms of their dialogue, you should pay the same kind of attention to the vocabulary of different age groups. A small child doesn't have the capacity to use long and obscure words in his speech, because he will never have heard or learned or understood them. Don't fall into the trap of crediting a child of, say, six or seven years old with words he would never say. It immediately damns your work in the eyes of the editor.

Listening to the chatter that occurs within your own family members is one of the simplest ways of sorting out the differing modes of dialogue. It wouldn't be fictional dialogue, but you would have a pretty clear idea of how characters address one another, and the kind of talk that occurs between various members and age groups.

Keep in mind too, that each individual reacts differently when addressing different people. Let's briefly invent a fictional teacher. He's thirty-eight years old, lives in a detached house in a nice neighbourhood, married, no children, keen on local affairs. He teaches at a large comprehensive school, with an allied junior school alongside.

When he admonishes the small child from the junior school (Example 1 below) he will speak in a different way from his speech to the insolent teenager (2). He will have a different rapport at home with his wife (3), and with the chairman of the committee meeting for the preservation of local environment he attends that evening (4).

Same character, four different modes of speech, depending very much on himself, but also on the age group and lifestyle of the people he addresses, and his relationship with each one. But through all this, you must keep his essential character the same, which is where the value of the detailed character study comes in.

More detailed information on this is given in another of my books in this series, *How to Create Fictional Characters*. So let's hear this character speak.

Examples

    1 'Not you again, young Kelly Warner! How many times must I tell you juniors not to run around corners? You're going to end up hurting yourself. Walk, don't run, my dear.'

    2 'Be in my office at four o'clock sharp, and no arguments, Cathcart. And you can get that mutinous look off your face, and don't even think of giving me any sob stories about having to get home on time. I've heard it all before.'

    3 'God, Helen, what a day. If I never had to go back to that jungle again, it would be too soon. Pour me a drink, there's a love.'

    4 'With respect, Mr Chairman, I'm sure the whole committee will agree that we simply have to do something now, or the whole infrastructure of the town is going to be damaged beyond repair.'

SENTENCE LENGTHS

You can vary the look of your dialogue considerably by the way you construct your sentences. Short, pithy sentences can be very emotive and give a sense of immediacy or urgency. Long, meandering sentences can sometimes be confusing for the reader, or they may hold up the action – and this may well be your intention. The teacher in the above examples spoke in a lengthier sentence to the chairman when he was trying to make an important point in the meeting. He could have made his speech shorter and more pedantic, but he probably wouldn't have got the attention of the others in the same way. It also made him sound as if he knew what he was talking about and had thought everything through.

To establish fear or shock, characters will usually speak in short, jerky sentences. In tender moments of comfort, love or condolence, the sentences will generally be longer, and the effect will be softer. It's an interesting exercise to study published novels to see how authors achieve these effects.

Try to vary the lengths of your sentences within any speech, and see the different effects you can create. If every sentence contains exactly the same number of words with the same number of syllables, you will end up producing an unfortunate sing-song effect.

Chapter 5

IT AIN'T WHAT YOU SAY . . .

It's the way that you say it . . . and never was anything more true. There are always occasions in real life when we wish we could take back the words we've just said. And not only the words themselves, but the hurtful way in which we've said them.

So this opens up a whole new avenue of thought for fictional dialogue. You can make your character say anything you want him to say, and in any way you choose to let him say it. You have total control over him . . . until the character screams at you that this isn't the way he'd yell at his wife, or slate his junior assistant, or kick his dog . . .

This should always be a good moment for you, because it means that your characters have become so real to you that you know exactly how they would react in certain situations. What you have to do now, is to put it across to your readers in the same precise way.

And however glamorous or wonderful it sounds when a more experienced author tells you the book virtually writes itself once the characters take over, you should still stay very much in control. It may be their story, but it's your book.

STRONG LANGUAGE AND WEAK DIALOGUE
No tough, hard-headed marine under fire would stop to consider the correct use of the Queen's English when speaking to his mates. And in fiction, this would be no time to be squeamish about writing the kind of words your tough marine would use.

This also involves not balking at the use of swear words or blasphemy, if that's the way they would react in a given situation. Nothing pin-points the amateur writer more accurately than the use of weak phrases such as 'Good heavens' or 'My word' or 'Goodness me' put into the mouth of some macho truck driver on the make, for instance.

Would an ambitious young guy, out on the town for the night, do anything other than invent some glamorous career for himself, in order to impress the young gullible girl he's after? Well, maybe he would, but if you are inventing a boastful young man who can see his cause vastly improved by such lies, then you have to put yourself into his mind and write his words in the way he would speak them.

It's regrettable to many people that the use of four-letter words has become so acceptable in our vocabulary nowadays, and obviously it's not compulsory to include them in your dialogue in order to sell your book. But however you have defined your characters, if you shy away from putting realistic dialogue into their mouths then they won't come across to your readers as authentic, believable people.

There's nothing new about using strong langauge in fiction. Nor was it always seen to be blasphemous or offensive in any way. In seventeenth and eighteenth century novels and plays, the word 'bloody' was used merely for emphasis.

'Bloody' has long been accepted as no more of an intensive form of expression than 'awfully', 'terribly' or 'fearfully', depending on the nature of the character who utters it. But if you, as a writer, object to its use, the answer is simple. Don't use it. But don't blunt the impact of your dialogue by using a softer word instead. Get around it in some other way.

Strong language can be achieved without always resorting to blasphemy. Strong fictional language can be interpreted as using the best and most emotive words you can to define strong characters, rather than weak, bland ones. Weak words indicate a weak character.

In the following scene from my 1920s novel, *To Love and Honour*, Daniel and his father are both strong characters, while Daniel's mother is dominated by her husband, and by far the weaker one of the three:

Daniel jumped up from the supper table.

'For God's sake! One minute you're accusing me of getting some girl into trouble, and the next you're as good as telling me to get on with it. There's no pleasing you, is there?'

Frank's bushy brows drew together in a fury.

'Don't you talk to me in those tones!' he bellowed. 'I'm still your father, whether you're twenty-two years old or not, and you'll treat me with respect.'

'A bit of respect from you wouldn't go amiss either,' Daniel snapped back.

'Stop it, both of you,' Helen's quiet voice broke in. 'Can't we have one meal without the two of you wrangling all the time? And can't you be pleased for Daniel that he's met a nice girl, Frank? I'm delighted, and I'll make her very welcome, darling.'

Frank turned his anger on her, his tone sneering.

'Well, no doubt you'll be singing a different tune if he marries her and brings her here to live. You'll be relegated to second place in your own kitchen then, Mother, and it's about the only place you'll have any say in things.'

'Shut up, can't you?' Incensed, Daniel put himself between his tearful mother and his father. 'I told you already I've only just met the girl and you're interfering already. If I ever ask her or anybody else to marry me, rest assured I'll never bring a wife to live under your roof!'

'And if you don't, you can say goodbye to your inheritance,' Frank put in triumphantly. 'There'll be no Roxy for you, boy. You'll be out on your own with your little bit of fluff, and you'll be barred from this house from then on. There'll be no little chit-chats with your mother again neither. How does that fit in with your plans, heh?'

61

'Daniel,' Helen said fearfully, 'your father means what he says. He always said that families should stick together – '

'Like one big happy family, you mean?' he said savagely.

No swear words are included in that scene, but the clash of characters is obvious, simply because Daniel faces up to his father and stands his ground. The mother's weaker character serves to underline the strength of the other two.

STILTED DIALOGUE

The worst thing an editor can say about your dialogue is that it's stilted or wooden. Some writers are confused as to exactly what is meant by the term. Quite simply, it usually means that your dialogue is stiff and unrealistic to the point of pomposity. Such comments would be pleasing enough if you were trying to portray a stiff and pompous character . . . but since they're usually said to an author who is trying to do just the opposite, they can be very crushing.

Stilted dialogue can occur when your speeches are pedantic, long-winded, too formal or over-correct for your characters. Very often a character will speak in a way that's quite unnatural to him, by using the lengthier negative form of the verbs instead of the shorter ones, which is more usual in direct speech.

In fictional dialogue, unless the speaker is an historical person who speaks in a fairly grand manner, the usual way is to shorten the negative form of the verbs. But again, it depends on the story. If you want to emphasise a speech, you may prefer to use the full expression, and there's also a case for using it to indicate a more emphatic negative.

Examples

'I have not got any money.'

or   'I haven't got any money.'

'I do not want to see my boyfriend tonight. We have not spoken for three days.'
or 'I don't want to see my boyfriend tonight. We haven't spoken for three days.'

'I did not tell him, because I could not bear the thought of him walking out on me.'
or 'I didn't tell him, because I couldn't bear the thought of him walking out on me.'

By shortening the negative forms of the verb, you also tighten up the writing and the reading becomes far smoother. Saying the dialogue out loud, or speaking it into a tape recorder, is a good way of testing whether or not your speeches are falling into the stilted trap.

Stilted speech can occur with the use of the irritating past perfect tense, the dreaded 'had had' when describing an event in the far past. I've generally used the 'had had' just once, and then gone into the simple past tense, and the intelligence of the reader puts the whole sequence into the correct perspective.

Example

'If I had had any idea what was going on, I'd have stopped it at once. But I didn't.'
'What could you have done?' he asked.
'I'd have gone straight to Julia with the information, and she wouldn't have stood for any of his nonsense.'

You could just as easily abbreviate the 'I had had' altogether, and simply say:

'If I'd had any idea what was going on, I'd have stopped it at once, but I didn't.' Et cetera.

Using long words simply to impress your readers when short

ones would do equally as well is another way of ending up with stilted dialogue. Your Victorian character might say the following:

> 'We're planning to attend the Chelsea Flower Show tomorrow. I'm told there's always a grand plethora of arrangements there.'

This kind of weighty wordage would be quite wrong for a modern girl of the 1990s, who would be more likely to say:

> 'We're off to the Chelsea Flower Show tomorrow. I'm told they always have a great show.'

The stilted effect is even more pronounced when the writer uses the character's name in every line of dialogue, as explained in Chapter 1.

> 'Shall we go out tonight, Lou?'
> 'Yes, John, that would be nice.'
> 'Where would you like to go then, Lou?'
> 'Oh, I'll leave it to you, John. I'm told the film at the Regal is very good, but you choose, John.'

AVOIDING REPEATED INFORMATION
If you are stating a fact in the text, there's no reason for qualifying it in dialogue, unless you are adding some new information to complement it. It's even worse to let your characters state the obvious in several different ways within the same speech. This will be seen by an editor as padding.

Examples

> **1** 'She's totally blind now. She can't see a thing, not even to read the newspaper or watch the tele-

vision. She's even lost the little bit of sight she had this time last year.'

If the character is totally blind, it should be obvious that she can't see at all, not even enough to read the newspaper or watch the television. The word 'totally' might also be considered unnecessary. The last sentence is superfluous. However, if this speech was broken up by another character enquiring about the person's blindness, the further sentences would be more acceptable, as follows:

2   'She's become totally blind now,' Dolly said.
    'How sad. Can't she see anything at all, not even to read the newspaper or watch the television?'
    'Not a thing,' Dolly went on. 'She's even lost the little bit of sight she had this time last year.'

3   'The girls said the hotel was going to be open from June this year. Well, they actually said June 4th, but George told me the brochure said the beginning of June. Or maybe he said the middle.'

In Example 3 the reader would be bored by having to read three sentences virtually saying the same thing, which results in making the information become too finicky. In real life, this is quite probably how we would go on about the hotel's opening, but in fiction it merely becomes fussy dialogue.

Sometimes repetition unwittingly occurs within phrases, as follows:

1   'I walked towards the stairs, while at the same time reading my book.'

2   'I was sufficiently near enough to him to see his nervous tic.'

3   'I'll begin first of all by telling you how difficult it's going to be.'

The unnecessary repetition occurs with (1) 'at the same time'; (2) 'sufficiently'; (3) 'first of all'.

DON'T JUST PASS THE SALT

Normal conversation between people can be incredibly boring when written down word for word. Try it and see. We all like to think we speak in scintillating fashion, and sometimes we do . . . but that's normally when we've had time to think about what we're going to say, or are out to impress, and however much we may deny it, we're all guilty of that at times.

But how about all those other times? When we're sitting on a train and feeling obliged to make small talk with the person sitting next to us, such as being trapped by a bore on an aeroplane; nagging the children to get them to school on a winter morning; those awful moments in a lift with one other person when it stops between floors; these are the times when conversational trivialities seem to be the only things to fill our heads, and they are exactly the type of trivialities to avoid in writing good fictional dialogue.

It is also when the ping-pong effect of speech shows up in these trivial exchanges. In the following examples, none of the comments do any of the jobs that dialogue is meant to do. It doesn't move the story forward, or show up character – except for being pretty boring speakers – or show any emotional state.

A passage containing the following dialogue would be construed as being a bit of static padding while the author decides how to get on with the story. It's the sort of easy, mindless breakfast chit-chat we might indulge in with our spouse. It may be fine for waking up slowly to another day, but good fictional dialogue it's not.

Example

    'I think it might rain today.'
      'Didn't it rain yesterday, or was it the day before?'
      'I can't remember now. Monday, I think.'

'Pass the milk, will you, Jim?'
'Here you are. More toast?'
'No thanks. We're nearly out of bread, anyway.'
'What, again?'
'Yes, I forgot to get another loaf yesterday.'

You may argue that this kind of chit-chat is sometimes heard on TV programmes and may well appear in TV scripts. It may even be heard on radio, to the appropriate accompaniment of sound effects.

But dialogue that's meant to be heard is not the same as dialogue that's meant to be read silently. In a novel, the above dialogue would be far too cosy and irritating, and would be holding up any real progress of the story. Between the pages of a book the dialogue needs to be more significant and forward-moving.

IT TAKES TWO TO DIALOGUE

Obviously, once you begin to use dialogue in your story, you are going to need more than one person on stage. Monologues and soliloquys don't fit into today's fiction. Each of your characters will be a foil to the other when they begin to converse with one another.

People don't always have to be verbally fighting with one another when they converse, but undoubtedly a good argument between two characters is one of the best ways of showing up their temperaments.

In the last chapter, the style of people's occupations and different age groups was mentioned. In the following examples, one of your characters is an elderly lady living in a retirement home. In each case, it wouldn't only be the elderly lady who reacted differently to the others. Each of the people with her would temper their speech accordingly.

Examples

1 'Come along now, Mary,' Matron said briskly. 'You can't stay in bed all day.'

'Why not, if I want to?' Mary retorted. 'I'm paying enough for this bed, and no pert young woman is going to tell me what to do.'

'Thanks for the compliment, but I do have qualifications for this job, you know – '

'And you're still a young chicken,' Mary went on. 'When you get to be five years off getting a telegram from the Queen like me, you can talk about being old. And I daresay by then you'll want to stay in bed all day too.'

2 'Are you really staying in bed all day, Great-Gran?' Marcus said admiringly, perched on the end of the bed so that he could stare at the wrinkled old skin more easily, and try to count the grooves.

Mary snorted. 'There's not much to get up for at my age, boy. The old legs don't work so well any more.'

'Can I try out your Zimmer frame?' he asked next.

She chuckled. 'Why not? The nurses will think it's me, and come running.'

'Will they tell you off?'

'Not me. I'm their oldest patient, see? They'll want to preserve me till I get my telegram from the Queen.'

'Like jam?' Marcus grinned.

3 'Now, Mother, you know you've got to get some exercise. It's bad for you to lie here all day,' Edward admonished her.

Mary glowered at him. When had he ever become so pompous? Retirement didn't suit him, and that last trip abroad with his prissy wife had put years on him. They hadn't thought of taking her with them, she thought nastily, her usual antagonism towards her son rearing up again.

'I'll lie here as long as I please, and no child of mine is telling me what to do.'

'I'm hardly a child. I turned seventy last birthday,' Edward said shortly.

'And I'm still your mother, and since neither you nor your wife wanted me to live with you I shall continue to do as I please.'

'You know it was only because of Fay's poor health – '

Mary smiled kindly. 'I do know, dear. And heaven help me from having to share a house with her. So we're all satisfied, aren't we?'

SAYING TOO MUCH, OR NOT ENOUGH

It's just as much a fault to shorten your characters' discussions to the point of brevity as it is to let them waffle on in what's commonly known as verbal diarrhoea. Don't be tempted to skim through the dialogue of an argument so that you fail to let it come to its logical and satisfactory conclusion. If you make such dialogue too short you will only leave readers feeling frustrated and annoyed.

Conversely, if you let the characters go on too long in any verbal exchange your readers will be bored, their attention will wander, and they will start skipping through your dialogue passages, and get on with the action in the story. Either that, or they'll be bored with the whole story and close the book.

Such decisions as to the length of each separate sequence of dialogue can only come from each author. But people sometimes question how much dialogue should be included in the whole book. Some writing tutors advocate that no more than a third of a novel should be given over to dialogue, and that this should be sprinkled throughout the book.

Like my father, I certainly agree that it should be sprinkled throughout the book, and about a third of a story is probably right. But it's impossible to generalise.

Reading other people's stories and novels can certainly give you good guidelines as to what's being accepted in today's market. Readers have always liked plenty of dialogue in fiction, and perhaps because of the influence of television drama these days, where conversational conflict is so important, they expect a good deal of it in their reading entertainment as well.

As well as the factual layout of dialogue and prose which you can see by reading published work, and the amount of dialogue that other authors (and publishers) have found acceptable, your own instinct should start to tell you when enough is enough in your own dialogue.

There's really no better way of getting the feel for realistic dialogue than just sitting down and writing scenes for yourself, revising wherever you think necessary, until your characters are saying exactly what you wanted them to say, as concisely and expressively as possible.

IS IT A CLICHÉ?

Every cliché was once beloved of past writers. It encapsulated everything they wanted to say so easily and explicitly. But once those well-known and self-explanatory phrases passed into the realm of familiarity, the use of the cliché was generally condemned by the literati.

But is it so wrong? Why shouldn't a character say 'it was as cold as charity last night', or 'it was as black as the ace of spades' or 'I couldn't see my hand in front of my face'? Why not indeed?

The simple fact is that clichés are far more acceptable when used in dialogue than in any other part of fiction. Used with discretion, I don't think they're so wrong anywhere in fiction, but that's a personal view.

But in dialogue, the cliché can come into its own – to use another cliché . . . In fact, a character who habitually speaks in clichéd terms assumes a certain personality. The smooth-talking lover who relies on tired and hackneyed lines to get his girl is one example. You *know* he's only out for what he can get.

Most of the phrases we now regard as clichés were once the invention of some clever person who saw the value in a euphemism. Some of those euphemisms have become appallingly trite, and never more so than when used in romantic fiction.

The 'bristling muscles' and 'hair-matted chests' of the heroes, and the 'china-blue eyes', 'silken skin' and 'tip-tilted nose' of the heroines are the type of clichés to make critics of the genre sneer.

Thankfully, not many of those phrases are likely to occur in dialogue, unless you really want to make your readers squirm by 'hearing' the hero tell his lover that she has skin as white as the driven snow . . . and most romantic novelists have long since avoided using them at all. Unfortunately, the myth persists that this is the kind of writing that all romantic novels contain.

But is it a cliché, or a simile? Why shouldn't a clever simile that likens one thing to another have its place in good writing? The author who invents his own similes can be said to be more creative than one who relies on the old reliable ones, but if a comparison defines something so accurately that it conjures up a picture in the mind, then I think it is valid to use it.

Who would not find any of the following snippets of dialogue acceptable when read in the context of the story in which they occur? Yet they all contain clichés:

1 'I can never tell the Jones boys apart. Just like peas in a pod they are,' Mrs Phillips said wonderingly.

2 'The smell coming from that factory was marvellous. It reminded me of new-mown hay.'

3 'If I had the chance,' sighed Amy, 'I'd give anything to be up there on the silver screen with Mr Douglas Fairbanks.'

3 'It was awful, Bert. When the police got there and broke open the door, it was obvious that the woman had shot him in cold blood,' Hilary said, shocked.

All the clichés used above express exactly what their authors are trying to say at that moment. They conjure up a picture and they appeal to the senses of the reader. Used selectively,

71

and especially when used in dialogue, the cliché is still alive and well.

Sometimes, in trying to be too literary and avoiding all those most useful little expressions and phrases, we can end up with the stilted and flat writing we all do our best to avoid.

Chapter 6

HE SAID, SHE SAID

One of the things that stamps the dialogue writer as an amateur is the constant use of adverbs to qualify the verb. They're not taboo, and sometimes they're necessary to show the reader exactly how your character is talking.

There are occasions when it's best to avoid the use of adverbs altogether, and some tutors will tell you that the dialogue should be able to stand alone, with nothing more than the unobtrusive 'he said'/'she said' to avoid the unwanted ping-pong effect. I don't entirely agree. I think much of the effect of the dialogue can be lost because the author is afraid of including an adverb, simply because he has been told to avoid its use.

It's quite true that when you read a scene of dialogue in a novel, you hardly notice 'he said' or 'she said'. Try it and see. Somehow, you get the effect of yourself reading the speech aloud, and the 'he said' et cetera becomes no more than an aside, to briefly identify the speaker. So far, so good.

If your character is speaking in violent tones, with his dialogue matching his temperament, you may not feel the need to qualify his speech at all. Adverbs can become intrusive. This is especially noticeable when the new writer constantly searches for alternatives, peppering the dialogue with ever-new and sometimes obsolete ones, mistakenly thinking he will enliven the text by doing so.

There is one well-known American writer who uses adverbs to the point of saturation, and it is an exercise in a kind of fascinated admiration to see how many different ones she can bring into a single book. It doesn't appear to have affected her sales, because the dialogue itself is so good.

So why not stick with 'he said'/'she said'? I would advise the occasional alternative, if only to bring variety into the writing. In my opinion, consistently using the same phrases, even to qualify speech, would simply be boring to read. Every book needs a sense of freshness about it, and it certainly won't help you to be published if you're predictable in plot, characters, dialogue, and everything else that goes to make up your story.

How many lectures have you listened to, how many How-To books have you read, where you are advised to be original as much as possible? Editors see so many unsolicited manuscripts that they inevitably see the same tired plots. They are inundated with the same descriptions of the same old characters, and probably cringe at some of the same old lines of dialogue. The author who can give them something fresh and original must stand a better chance of at least a second reading.

However, there is a strong case for using the simple form of 'he said'/'she said' when you feel it's the only thing that's needed. Its value is that it effectively fades into the background and doesn't deter the reader from the important part of the speech. In the end, it's up to you how often you use it. All I would say is, don't do it all the time. Be varied. Be original.

EFFECTIVE ADVERBS
A simple sentence of dialogue can be expressed as follows:

> 'We won't do the art gallery tonight. It's better left
> until tomorrow,' Joe said.

This is bland, straightforward and could mean anything. Naturally, by the time you reached this line of dialogue in a story, you would know very well who Joe was, and his reason for deciding not to do the art gallery tonight, but to leave it until tomorrow. But supposing that this piece of dialogue was standing alone, or even forming the opening to a short story or novel. Then the meaning you convey in even the simplest of sentences can be completely changed by the use of a qualifying and effective adverb:

> 'We won't do the art gallery tonight. It's better left until tomorrow,' Joe said kindly/gently/considerately.

Is this the caring grandson, accompanying his grandmother on a trip to London? Could be.

> 'We won't do the art gallery tonight. It's better left until tomorrow,' Joe said meaningly/aggressively/forcefully.

Is this the crook, informing his mates that tomorrow would be a better night for breaking into the art gallery?

> 'We won't do the art gallery tonight. It's better left until tomorrow,' Joe said hopefully.

Whoever Joe is in this sentence, he's probably already worn out with all that trudging about.

Look ahead from this last brief entry into the character's mind. Maybe Joe's reluctance will persuade his girlfriend to 'do' the art gallery on her own, with whatever consequences you devise. A romantic background might result in the heroine meeting someone else. A more sinister one could result in her being involved in a crime, without Joe's protection.

As well as showing exactly what you mean by the use of a qualifying adverb, you also define the character's mood more clearly at that precise moment. An effective sequence of dialogue is one that incorporates several methods of showing who is speaking, and thereby demonstrating his or her present attitude, as has been shown in any of the examples in previous chapters. So don't despise the adverb . . .

When you use a character-descriptive adverb, you instantly put expression into your reader's mind as he reads the lines of dialogue. It's almost impossible to read a piece of dialogue that is clearly qualified in this way, without automatically putting the right connotation into your own mind. Some effective, most-used character-descriptive adverbs for qualifying 'he said'/'she said' speeches are as follows:

accurately	admiringly	aggressively	airily
amiably	angrily	arrogantly	automatically
baldly	belatedly	bitterly	blandly
blithely	boastfully	bravely	bullishly
calmly	calculatingly	callously	clearly
coldly	coolly	crossly	crushingly
darkly	desperately	disbelievingly	discreetly
dryly	drowsily	dully	dutifully
easily	earnestly	edgily	effusively
engagingly	enjoyably	enigmatically	excitedly
fairly	faintly	fitfully	flatly
fleetingly	flirtily	forcefully	freely
gaily	gamely	genteelly	glibly
grandly	gravely	guardedly	gutterally
happily	haltingly	haughtily	heatedly
hedgily	hoarsely	hopefully	humorously
icily	immediately	immodestly	impertinently
impotently	instantly	irritably	invitingly
jadedly	jauntily	jerkily	jokily
jovially	joyously	jubilantly	justifiably
keenly	killingly	kindly	kind-heartedly
kittenishly	knavishly	knowingly	knowledgeably
laboriously	lastly	laudably	laughingly
leeringly	lightly	loosely	lovingly

maddeningly	malevolently	meanly	melodiously
modestly	moodily	mournfully	murderously
nastily	naughtily	neatly	nervously
nicely	noisily	nonchalantly	numbly
obediently	objectively	obscenely	obscurely
offensively	officiously	optimistically	outrageously
painfully	patiently	pathetically	paradoxically
placidly	prettily	primly	pompously
quaintly	qualmishly	quarrelsomely	quaveringly
queerly	quellingly	querulously	quietly
racily	radiantly	raunchily	rationally
reasonably	regretfully	roundly	rudely
sadly	saliently	saucily	savagely
scratchily	secretly	shiftily	spitefully
tacitly	tactfully	tautly	tenderly
tightly	thankfully	thinly	touchily
ubiquitously	unabatedly	unanswerably	unbearably
uncomfortably	unconcernedly	uncouthly	unkindly
vacantly	vainly	valiantly	vapidly
vehemently	victoriously	violently	vulgarly
waggishly	warmly	waspishly	weakly
wearily	woefully	wonderingly	wryly
yearningly	yieldingly	youthfully	
zanily	zealously	zestfully	

There are thousands more. Each of them will betray something more about the character who is speaking than the simple 'he said'/'she said'.

PASSIVE AND ACTIVE VERBS
Along with all the ways already mentioned to define the way your characters speak, don't ignore the use of passive and active verbs. There are also the verbs that I call 'uppers and

downers'. These have nothing to do with pep pills or tran-
quillisers, but convey exactly what they mean by their individual sounds.

One of my particular 'downers' is the word 'explained'. To
me, this has a flat, slightly condescending sound (hence
'downer'), while 'exclaimed' has an upbeat, buoyant sound.
'Explained' would be a passive word in my opinion, while
'exclaimed' is an active one. You only have to say the words
aloud to hear the difference.

Of course, there may be many occasions when you want
your characters to explain something to someone else, but be
sure when you use the phrase 'he explained' that you're not
putting a subtly pompous note into the dialogue.

You may disagree with my theory on word sounds, since the
interpretation of any word is a personal thing. But, just as you
should try to 'hear' your characters' dialogue in your head, you
should also hear the *way* that your characters speak, and try to
get those nuances across to the reader in the clearest possible
way.

In the previous chapter, the scene from *To Love and Honour* demonstrates various mixes of passive and active verbs
and qualifying adverbs.

Basically, the passive verb is more static, softer in tone,
and somewhat understated. It doesn't intrude or define as
much as its louder counterpart, the active verb, which shows
more movement, and is often of an aggressive nature. The
active verb is also more visually descriptive. You mentally
'see' as well as 'hear' the character's tone of voice.

My choice of some passive verbs is as follows:

affirmed	allowed	asked	averred
breathed	called	claimed	coaxed
cried	debated	demurred	grumbled
guessed	hazarded	hedged	interjected
lisped	mouthed	murmured	opined
pouted	promised	queried	reasoned
rejoined	remonstrated	said	spoke
stated	vowed		

Active verbs are stronger in tone:

argued	bellowed	blathered	blazed
chaffed	demanded	dictated	flared
fumed	gabbled	grated	griped
howled	laughed	leered	marvelled
mocked	raged	roared	screamed
shouted	shrieked	slurred	snapped
sneered	squealed	stormed	stuttered
swore	taunted	wept	wheezed
whined	yapped	yawned	yelled

It's easy enough to register the different tone of voice in each of the following pieces of dialogue, and to interpret where the character might be in different situations:

> 'Will you please let me go?' she said.
> 'Will you please let me go?' she said angrily.
> 'Will you please let me go?' she said fearfully.
> 'Will you please let me go?' she snapped.
> 'Will you please let me go?' she screamed.
> 'Will you please let me go?' she mouthed.
> 'Will you please let me go?' she wept.

Many verbs have a noun as their root, including some of those above. Some authors invent their own descriptive verbs by employing a less usual noun to do the job, such as 'she crisped'. Literary purists would undoubtedly object, but since writing is very much a personal and individual craft, it's up to you to decide whether or not you like this style of writing.

SPEECHES – BEGINNINGS AND ENDINGS
Where you begin and end a piece of dialogue can be just as important as the dialogue itself. It can change your meaning considerably if you begin it in the wrong place, and perhaps end on a weaker note than you intended.

Just as you should always try to 'hear' your characters

speaking their lines of dialogue, it always helps to have a visual image of them in your mind as well. Imagine that precocious ten-year-old strutting across the school playground as you give her her words to say. Try to see the old man trying vainly to cross a busy street and asking for help, and all these little tricks will help you to get their dialogue more accurate.

Carry this visual image further by giving an impression of what they're actually doing while they're talking. Remember that most people don't stand like statues when they talk. Dialogue and action complement each other.

At a party people will usually have drinks in their hands, and be juggling with paper plates and/or handbags. At a race meeting your heroine may be conscious that she's worn the wrong shoes, and that her heels are sinking into the mud while she's trying to make an impression on the guy she's just met. Your crook may be conscious of the sweat trickling down his back as he hears the creak of a door somewhere in the building he thought was deserted. Use all this visual information to further the effect of your dialogue and subtly set your scenes in the reader's mind.

The examples below show effective ways of beginning and ending such speeches with interspersing action. Each pair of examples demonstrate how the sentences can be strengthened or made more effective by paying some attention to where the speeches begin and end in order to enhance their dramatic effect. In some cases it's a part of the entire speech that is improved by breaking it up, and not the entire sequence. Any of the examples is an adequate piece of dialogue, and would depend on the scene of which they are a part, and on how you want to sharpen your characterisation at that point.

1 'I don't care what old Grimsby says,' Tess said, tossing her pony-tail as she strutted across the playground. 'I'm not doing any more homework and that's that.'
2 Tess tossed her pony-tail as she strutted across the playground. 'Well, I'm not doing any more

80

homework and that's that. I don't care what old Grimsby says.'

3 'You bastard!' Tom Oakley wheezed, waving his stick wildly at the speeding car on the busy main road. 'You nearly had me down then. A couple of years' National Service is what you buggers need –'
4 'You nearly had me down then, you bastard!' Tom Oakley wheezed, waving his stick wildly at the speeding car on the busy main road. 'A couple of years' National Service is what you buggers need –'

5 'God, why did I wear these flimsy things?' Sheila said, feeling her heels slowly sinking into the racecourse mud. 'I feel such an idiot, and you're not helping!'
6 'I feel such an idiot in these flimsy things,' Sheila said, feeling her heels slowly sinking into the racecourse mud. 'And you're not helping!'

7 'Did you hear that?' Bert said, the sweat trickling down his back in the dusty atmosphere of the warehouse. 'I swear I heard a door creak just then.'
    Jack grunted. 'You're getting yellow, mate. The place is empty and we ain't going to be disturbed tonight.'
8 'I swear I heard a door creak just then. Did you hear that?' Bert said, the sweat trickling down his back in the dusty atmosphere of the warehouse.
    'The place is empty and we ain't going to be disturbed tonight. You're getting yellow, mate,' Jack grunted.

Particularly in the last pair of examples above, the tension is increased in 7, since the reader would pause to try to 'hear' what Bert heard before he actually mentioned the door creaking. Jack's speech ends with the sure indication to the reader that they *are* going to be disturbed tonight.

Winding up a speech successfully avoids the inclination to let your characters go on too long. Knowing where a speech should end comes partly through instinct, and partly by the sheer look of the page. Just don't let your speeches be too long, and make your characters intelligent enough to know when to wind things up at the best point that they can. If all else fails, since you should be mentally getting under the skin of all your characters, tell yourself not to be a bore, and stop.

USING NAMES AS FLAGS
Beginning a character's dialogue by letting him name the other person is the obvious way of telling the reader to whom he's speaking. It also supplies emphasis, both to the speaker and his companion. A schoolteacher's dialogue, of the kind that we all surely remember, might go like this:

> 'Harry Jones, come out to the front this minute!' Miss Leaver said. 'And Philippa Daley, I'll see you after class.'

Both the child characters assume a certain importance in having their names mentioned in full. We just know that they're socially disruptive or just plain naughty, and that they're going to get their come-uppance from the teacher.

Without knowing anything else about them, we can sympathise, and maybe have a grudging admiration for Harry Jones and Philippa Daley, and wonder what they could have done to cause ructions in the classroom. Whatever it was, they're obviously not wimpish characters, or they wouldn't have been singled out in such a way. And all this is implied from the use of their full names at the beginning of the dialogue.

You could argue that this is the normal way for a teacher to single out two children from a large class. But the speech would have lost some of its impact, and the characters their importance, if she had put their full names at the end of the sentences, as follows:

> 'Come out to the front of the class, Harry Jones,'

Miss Leaver said. 'And I'll see you after class, Philippa Daley.'

As writers, we don't expect readers to analyse every line of dialogue or style of writing. Nor should they. Their job is to read and enjoy the books, and it's our job to make the reading as smooth and pertinent as we can.

A romantic novel often includes the hero calling the heroine by her full name at certain moments. It's a trick I have used fairly often. There's no logical reason why it should be effective, but it is, as long as it's done sparingly.

You will find the same trick used in countless books, and in films too. I only have to remember John Wayne's Western voice to recall him frequently calling his screen wife Mrs Whatever. It definitely has a certain charm about it.

And Mr Bennett in *Pride and Prejudice* consistently called his wife Mrs Bennett. This would obviously be an old-fashioned method to employ now, but just as in the John Wayne films, it gave weight and dignity to her personality.

Using a character's name as a flag – or an introduction – to the dialogue is also a useful way of naming them smoothly. Imagine the sound of a doorbell ringing, and our hero going to answer it.

'Imogen! Good Lord, after all these years. It must
be fate that you've turned up tonight of all nights.
Come on in and join the party.'

This mini-piece of dialogue sets an entire scene. The unexpected guest is probably going to be thrown off-balance by walking into a party, and maybe the other guests are going to be disturbed by her appearance too. Or maybe not. Such an outcome depends on the plot of the story. But most importantly out of this small piece of dialogue, the reader has learned the newcomer's name, and it's pretty obvious that the hero once knew her well, if he can remember her instantly from years back.

Using Imogen's name as the flag to the dialogue should also mean that she has some important future role to play in the story. Don't throw such flags in indiscriminately. Make them work for you.

You always know the moment in a TV soap when a new character is going to be introduced. The other characters throw in a hitherto unknown name from time to time, until it becomes familiar. A long-lost son or daughter or cousin or previous fiancée is about to turn up out of the blue, and the viewer has been prepared for it by hearing the name a few times. If it sometimes stretches the credibility as to how many of these long-lost attachments can turn up, well, that's show business. But the same idea can be used in fiction.

Characters who are destined to appear later in your book can be mentioned, in whatever mood you may want your other characters to remember him, through the dialogue of those other characters. Establish the name, and something about him, and he won't appear as such a shock when he eventually arrives on the scene.

> 'I still miss our Matt,' Evie said wistfully. 'I can hardly believe he's been gone nearly five years. I wonder if he'll ever come back.'
>
> 'He always said he would, Mother,' Philip said, trying to cheer her up. 'And didn't you always say he'd turn up again like the proverbial bad penny someday, just when we least expect him?'

Using Matt's name as a flag in a dialogue like this is a sure sign that he's going to turn up sooner or later. You also have a small clue as to his character to arouse your curiosity. Was he as bad a penny as the cliché implies? Or was this just a familiar way of referring to a long-lost son?

Using a name at the beginning of a sentence also underlines the feeling of anger, shock, disappointment or delight on the part of the speaker. At the same time it strengthens the action of the named person.

> 'David, how could you be so cruel?'
> 'Lucy, it's you!'

'Anne, I never thought you could be so petty.'
'Geoff, the flowers were a lovely surprise!'

WRITING VISUALLY

This is the fiction writer's most valuable asset. It also employs the technique of going straight for the senses. Letting your readers see/hear/taste/smell things the way you want them to should be every author's aim.

Apart from writing straight description, using dialogue is one of the simplest ways of writing visually, since you have plenty of opportunity for letting the characters converse about any kind of event or memory, for as long as it's feasible to keep a conversation alive. Don't waste it.

'Do you remember that night on the beach in St Ives?' Julie said, her eyes full of dreams.

'Which one?' Eddie teased her.

'Oh, you know very well which one! The best one! We'd watched the fishing boats coming in, and we bought those wonderful fresh-caught mackerel – '

'Of course I remember. We built a bonfire on the beach when it got dark and cooked them. The taste of them was out of this world.'

Julie grinned. 'Even though you complained all the time about the sand being so gritty, and the wine not being cool enough in the last heat of the day?'

'Even so,' Eddie said softly.

A dialogue scene like that conjures up a picture without going into long narrative passages of two people sharing a picnic on a Cornish beach. In essence, it was no more than that, but the dialogue between the two of them brings the scene and the memories vividly to mind. You don't need to know Cornwall intimately, or to have a travelogue description of the town of St Ives, to experience the romance of that particular night.

When you write such scenes, you should always put your-self into the picture. The author is a kind of silent observer/participant, taking a vicarious look into other people's lives, and listening in on private conversations. The best part of it is, you can make those conversations go any way you please. You can create the best – or worst – kinds of memories to enhance and enrich your plot.

Writing visually also means trying to see your scenes as if they're moving pictures inside your head. You will allow your readers to see your heroine's sun-kissed hair swinging in the breeze far more easily if you can see it yourself. Be aware of movement when you write your scenes, and that sense of movement will come through in your dialogue.

VERBAL FIGHTS

An argument between your characters can be anything you want it to be. It can be dramatic and earth-shattering, threatening to break up a marriage or push the button on the bomb . . . or it can be sweetly domestic, meaningless in terms of great up-heavals, showing up the speakers' strengths in their own security.

Arguments can be challenging, pushing your characters into places and tight corners where they don't want to be. They can be demoralising and humiliating, and totally destroy a relationship between two people.

They can certainly be some of the most satisfying scenes for an author to write, and the author who holds back on writing such scenes with gusto is missing out on the enjoy-ment of writing such scenes. Since every novel or story must contain some kind of conflict to be interesting, verbal fights can underline that conflict most effectively.

It's no accident that the most memorable scenes in novels and films are those in which the characters are quarrelling or in strong conflict with one another. It's human nature to be inquisitive, to argue, to air opinions, to be as bitchy as a situation demands. All fiction reflects human nature, and it's a total waste of such conflict if it's merely reported in the text, without giving readers the benefit and added excitement of 'enjoying' those fights.

There are many examples already given in previous chapters. I would just reiterate that every dramatic and often highly emotional scene of dialogue deserves as much writing and rewriting as is necessary. Only by trial and error can you begin to realise your own potential as a writer.

And if you're not satisfied with your first – or your tenth – draft, you can always throw it into the wastepaper basket and start again. It goes with the job.

Chapter 7

THE LISTENING EAR

A writer should not only be an observer of all human life, but very definitely a listener too. Television is a huge help to the writer looking for new ideas, because we can get a flavour of every kind of lifestyle imaginable, and hear a great variety of dialogue.

We can see exactly how MPs behave in the House of Commons, and learn the forms of address that they use. Through the many documentaries that are shown we can see the differences in our way of life, and, say, the American way. Same language, different lifestyles, and in some cases, vastly different speech styles.

Programmes such as *Lovejoy*, *Minder*, *Spender* and all the various soap operas give us the kind of dialogue that people of different classes and walks of life use. There is a surfeit of Australian and American soap operas on our screens, and even if you don't care for them, they are ready-made sources of idioms if you want to write about Australian or American characters.

Class differences will always exist, and should be exploited to the full in the dialogue your characters use. 'People differences' exist too, because no two people can ever envisage things in exactly the same way. However compatible they may seem, one speaker will always have the edge on the other, whether it's in status, age, beauty, wealth, intelligence, gender, and so on. Make your dialogue sparkling enough to define such differences wherever necessary.

RADIO AND DRAMA TECHNIQUES

Fiction in short stories and novels is primarily intended to be read silently by one person at a time. You may think you're doing a great job in making your dialogue as real as you can, but in the end, it's the reader who will put all the inflexion into the dialogue you write, interpreting the speeches in his or her own way, no matter how much you have strived to make it accurate. But as far as possible you obviously want that reader to see and hear your characters as you see them.

A good way to test any fictional dialogue is to think of it in radio and drama terms. Even if you are writing in novel or short story form, this is the keenest way to 'hear' if your dialogue is successful.

The reason should be obvious. Radio is perhaps the most taxing of all drama mediums. You don't have the added advantage of seeing the actors, as you do in a stage or television play. You have none of the facial expressions or body language to support your dialogue. It must stand alone, with no more than the actors' interpretation to complement your words.

If you were to strip away every bit of additional wordage from a scene of your own dialogue, ideally you should still be able to 'see' and 'hear' the characters. The extra wordage is part of the format of novel fiction, and a book would be thinner in every way without it, but by trying to assess the dialogue you write without all those extras, you will prove its strength – or its weakness.

The following scene is an illustration of this. Example 1 is the way it would be done in a novel. Example 2 is a simplified version, showing the dialogue only, without the extra trappings. Example 1 is clearly the better one to use in a novel, when both writer and reader have the time to explore characters and plot thoroughly.

In a radio play, the characters' body movements and thought processes are not available, and neither is the advantage of the tone of voice through speech verbs or adverbs. The strength of the dialogue must come from the characters' words themselves. By stripping away all these extras as in

Example 2 of the same scene, you would show up any flaws in the dialogue.

1   Mather looked the youth over with a growing feeling of annoyance. He blew smoke from his cigar into the air with an arrogant puff of his cheeks.

'You're far too young for this job,' he snapped. 'Who sent you to me?'

The boy shifted nervously. It hadn't been his idea to come in the first place. His probation officer had thought it would be good training . . .

'Mr Peacock – '

Mather snorted derisively.

'Dear God, preserve me from do-gooders. Well, boy, do you think you can handle the job? It means a lot of heavy lifting, and you look as though a strong wind would blow you away.'

Alan clenched his hands. Nobody knew how desperately he needed this job.

'I'm a bloody sight stronger than I look – Sir,' he muttered, thinking privately he'd like to get this pompous jerk down an alley on a dark night and prove his point.

2   'You're far to young for this job. Who sent you to me?'

'Mr Peacock – '

'Dear God, preserve me from do-gooders. Well, boy, do you think you can handle the job? It means a lot of heavy lifting, and you look as though a strong wind would blow you away.'

'I'm a bloody sight stronger than I look – Sir.'

Example 2 gives the bare bones of the dialogue between the characters, but doesn't fully flesh it out. Even so, it is powerful enough to stand alone, if required. It successfully defines the roles of the two speakers, and the differences between them in status and ages, which would be the object of the brief rewrite of this scene. You can often see where an extra word or two injected into your speeches will make all the difference to your original intention.

As another illustration of the usefulness of this exercise, imagine the same scene in a novel, written with far less attention to character identification. In Example 3 we're told that Mather is impatient, and that the boy is aggressive, but it doesn't come through in their dialogue.

3   Mather looked the youth over with a growing feeling of annoyance. He blew smoke from his cigar into the air with an arrogant puff of his cheeks.

'You're too young for this job. Who sent you to me?'

The boy shifted nervously. It hadn't been his idea to come in the first place. His probation officer had thought it would be good training . . .

'Mr Peacock.'

Mather snorted derisively.

'I see. Do you think you can handle the job? It means a lot of heavy lifting, and you don't look too strong.'

Alan clenched his hands. Nobody knew how desperately he needed this job.

'I'm stronger than I look, Sir,' he muttered, thinking privately he'd like to get this pompous jerk down an alley on a dark night and prove his point.

Neither of these two characters comes across as forcefully in this scene. Even though the 'extras' are virtually the same, the dialogue is weakened and is more bland. Example 4 shows it up.

4   'You're too young for this job. Who sent you to me?'

92

'Mr Peacock.'

'I see. Do you think you can handle the job? It means a lot of heavy lifting, and you don't look too strong.'

'I'm stronger than I look, Sir.'

As with all kinds of writing, the best way of researching a market is to study it. If you want to write for radio, there's no substitute for listening to radio plays and seeing how your peers create characters literally out of thin air. In radio, it's down to the listeners to supply all the accoutrements for the characters that the author creates. They flesh them out, simply from the voices they hear, and the words that the characters are given to say.

Radio is a very spare medium to write for. There's no opportunity in it for wasted words. Everything that is heard must be meaningful and move the story along. Each of the characters must be instantly recognisable, with his own voice, and it's fatal to rely solely on the actors that you hope will be cast in your play.

The actors' names are the ones that will inevitably end up being better known than your own, but it's the writer who provides them with their lines to say. It should be the writer's intent to make those characters so distinctive that casting becomes secondary, at least to you.

You may be thrilled to think that Dame Judi Dench or David Jason is going to play one of your characters. But if you don't give those characters the right kind of dialogue to say in the first place, it's unlikely that your play will get beyond a first reading.

Writing for radio, as for no other medium, means that character-building relies heavily on dialogue. When you have written a story or play for radio, record it if you can, and try listening to it with your eyes closed. Just as a blind person develops extra senses, this small trick of concentrated listening will help you to pick up all the dialogue flaws that you might otherwise miss.

Remember that if your character is a teenager she would speak in a bright, youthful way. A child may stammer, using simpler words than his adult companions. A forceful man will speak in forceful tones, using forceful words. A dreamy, older woman's dialogue would be gentler and more loosely structured, simply because of her personality. Always keep in mind that dialogue is a key to character, and that character is enhanced by dialogue.

Radio dialogue is rarely prolonged. A page of radio script is full of short sentences that read unlike the dialogue in novel fiction. It may seem terse at first reading, but since it's meant to be read aloud without any narrative to back it up, every word must count. The following short scene would be supported by sound effects, both in the script and the final production, but essentially it's the dialogue that carries the story along.

'Have you brought the stuff, Briggs?'
'I'm not stupid enough to forget it. It's over there, in the corner.'
'I'll check it before we go – '
'What's the matter, don't you trust me even now?'
'When I was inside I learned never to trust any-one, and I don't aim to start now.'
'Is that right? Maybe it's a pity we began this little caper at all then. It ain't too late to back out now – and without me fronting you – '
'Don't be such a damn fool, Briggs.'

Add to these sentences a sharp, authoritative voice for one character, and a coarse, guttural one for the other, and nothing more is needed to tell the listener that here are two villains intent on some crime or other. From these few sentences, the listener knows that at least one of them has been in prison, and that neither really trusts or likes the other. The use of the surname from the first speaker also implies the feeling of dislike and superiority. Such information is smoothly and easily injected into the listener's mind by the words that the characters use.

LISTEN TO TV/RADIO VOICES

We're very fortunate in having such a wealth of media talent on our doorsteps, and right inside our homes, through the media of radio and TV. It's no problem to know how a weatherman speaks, or a game-show host, or the confident exponent of a thousand other different occupations. Documentaries will provide you with the kind of people who do great things for the environment or drift into crime, or behave in the classrooms, as will children's TV programmes such as *Grange Hill*.

Don't waste such ready-made market research, nor ignore all the marvellous voices that have come into our living-rooms over the years. If you have difficulty creating a voice for a crusty old colonel, for instance, you might remember the voice of Gilbert Harding. If you want a heroine who's delightfully uppercrust, you might call up Penelope Keith's voice.

I am not advocating basing your fictional characters directly on people in the public eye. But all the characters you create are made up of a mixture of people you know, your own ideals, opinions and hang-ups, as well as a uniqueness to every one of them that comes from your imagination.

And if one of your problems with character-building is getting the dialogue right, then there's nothing wrong with thinking of a well-known personality whose voice and attitudes coincide with the way you perceive your character. Putting 'that voice' into your character's mouth may just be the key to letting her say exactly what you wanted her to say.

FASCINATING BUS QUEUES

Who would not be an eavesdropper? Who can resist it? Some of the sauciest, most intriguing and irritating conversations can be overheard while waiting for a bus or a train, or standing in a queue at the supermarket checkout. They can irritate you because as you were dying to hear the rest of it, the bus or train comes along, or it's your turn at the checkout, and short of asking what happened next, you've got no option but to move along.

But how about those half-heard conversations? If they were intriguing enough to catch your interest, wouldn't they be interesting enough to incorporate in a story? I'm not suggesting you stand by with a tape-recorder bugging private conversations, but there's nothing to stop you taking the germ of a conversation and turning it into an idea for a story, or a starting point for a scene of dialogue.

You would almost certainly want to doctor the orginal a little, especially if it was slightly risqué, but it's a fact that few people ever recognise themselves in a story, let alone are able to pin-point an exact piece of dialogue as something they once said.

In any case, unless you are so foolish as to make it blatantly obvious that your story is about the woman next door who ran off with the milkman, the people who think that a story is written about them almost always see themselves as the hero, and rarely as the villain.

One of my own teenage novels grew from a snippet of conversation I overheard. It was a mother sending her child to buy something at the corner shop, and telling him not to come back if he lost the money. It was the kind of harmless remark that mothers say without thinking, and is not meant to be taken seriously.

But it got me thinking. A small child doesn't always understand that a mother's careless remark is only said as an 'aside'. What mother in her right mind would expect or want such a small child to run off if he lost some money? But what if a child in a story *did* take such a remark seriously? What if he *did* lose the money, and got so scared he *didn't* come back . . .?

The novelist's essential 'what-if' questions in my mind began my plot machinations working. My child character would be a small boy, and the 'mother' of the original conversation was to turn into his teenage sister who was reluctantly looking after him for the evening, though she'd much prefer to have been spending the time alone with her boyfriend. The idea was to be incorporated into a teenage novel.

The characters of the teenage sister and irritating small brother were well established before the original trigger of the overheard dialogue entered the plot. This is how it eventually came out in *Roses All The Way* (Jean Saunders, Heinemann Pyramid Books):

I stuck my head out of the back door and yelled for Jamie to come in for a minute. He still had that mutinous look on his face, which I ignored.

'I want you to go down to the corner shop and get a medium sliced loaf,' I instructed. 'Can you remember that or shall I write it down?'

'Why do I have to go all the time?' he grumbled. 'I don't *have* to just because you say so.'

Out of the corner of my eye I could see Dave grinning, and I was damned if I was going to stand for any cheek from a seven-year-old kid in front of him.

'Look, you'll just do as you're told, and be quick about it,' I snapped. 'Or I'll tell Charlie what a little pig you are sometimes. Dave's staying to tea, and we're having baked beans on toast, so if you want any, you'll have to get the bread. *Jamie!*'

I yelled again as he stood there glaring at me from under his sandy eyebrows. God, he could be as stubborn as a locked door without a key when he wanted to be.

'All right, I'm going!' he yelled back, his face red and furious.

'And don't you dare come back here if you lose that money,' I shouted after him, as he stuffed the little red purse in his shorts pocket. He slammed the back door in reply.

A few paragraphs later came the line of dialogue at the end of the chapter that began all the doubts in the sister's mind, and also in the reader's.

'Jamie's been gone a hell of a long time just to get a loaf of bread,' I said uneasily.

I'm not saying that you can always see the potential for an entire novel out of a piece of overheard conversation. But it's quite useful to keep a jottings book for any interesting snippets that you hear. When you look through them at some later stage, you may be pleasantly surprised at the way they can provide you with an idea for a story.

THE INTERRUPTED SPEECH
In most stories you will come across the interrupted speech at some point or other. It happens quite often in romantic novels. Just as the hero or heroine is about to reveal the very thing that will clarify all their misunderstandings, the telephone will ring, or someone will arrive unexpectedly. They will frequently be interrupted in their attempts at lovemaking, to the frustration of characters and readers alike.

Unfortunately this device can be overdone to the point of a really heavy contrivance. It can be useful, but try to make those interruptions feasible and not farcical.

OVERLOADED SPEECHES
Making your speeches ponderously long is a sure way of making your reader's attention wander. In real life, our eyes go glazed when we're trapped in the corner of a room with a boring speaker who goes on and on and on . . . and it's no different in fiction. Keep the conversation sparkling and no one will be bored.

Overloaded speeches will occur if you let one character go on for too long without intervention or comment by someone else. The very nature of dialogue is a conversation, not a monologue.

Think about someone you know who will never let you get a word in edgeways. We all know someone like that. Don't you wish him to Kingdom Come when you're simply dying to express an opinion of your own that may be just as pertinent as his?

Share your dialogue out between the characters, though never in exactly equal measure. If you did so, it would be as predictable and boring as having one speaker taking over the whole time, while leaving the other with nothing to say.

Another slant on overloading your speeches is the irritation of giving out unnecessary information. This includes letting one character tell the other something of which he is obviously well aware. It's the mark of the amateur, and it's called padding:

> 'I saw your June the other day, Mark.'
> 'June, my sister?'
> 'That's right,' Bill said. 'Didn't she go to Enfield for a while to work with that friend of hers?'
> Mark nodded. 'My sister June always wanted to get away from here, and so did her friend, Linda. They both hated working at Wyatt's.'
> 'Oh, you mean Wyatt's in the High Street?'

Having read this far through this book, I hope by now that this kind of dialogue seems ridiculously elaborate to you. Unfortunately, it occurs often enough in unpublished manuscripts. It's very ponderous and clumsy, simply because the writer is attempting to clarify everything in the finest detail. As it stands, there's just too much clutter in it.

Although you don't want to clip everything down to the barest essentials, at least give the reader credit for using her own imagination and intelligence. A better and tighter phrasing of this dialogue would be as follows:

> 'I saw your sister June the other day, Mark.'
> 'Did you?'
> Bill nodded. 'Didn't she go to Enfield for a while to work with that friend of hers?'
> 'Yes, June and Linda always wanted to get away from here. They both hated working at Wyatt's in the High Street.'

There's no need to elaborate further. One mention that June is Bill's sister is enough. One mention of Wyatt's location if it's important, is enough. We know that Linda is her friend, and there's no need to tell us twice.

Such overloading of redundant facts holds up the flow of the conversation. Dialogue will undoubtedly make your novel easier on the eye and easier to read. It will fill your book with less effort than writing pages and pages of narrative. But if it's over-informative to the point of fussiness, then it won't 'sound' right to your reader, and it just won't work.

So don't fall into the trap of filling in every tiny bit of domestic information that you can, simply to use up the required number of words for your story.

Gaynor Davies, the fiction editor of *Woman's Weekly*, calls this info-padding 'butler-and-maiding', which seems a particularly expressive phrase. It also indicates that editors are well used to seeing such excesses in the writing.

To sum up – writing dialogue for dialogue's sake alone will not make your book more interesting. In an earlier chapter, I suggested that you might look at prose scenes in your book and see where they could be lifted by using dialogue instead. Used with common sense and discretion, that idea holds good, providing you don't kill the impact by repeating information that is going to stall the action.

SAYING IT OUT LOUD

Although it has been suggested that you read your dialogue aloud to test it, remember what was said at the beginning of this chapter. The dialogue that you write for a novel is not really meant to be read aloud. It's intended to be read silently and privately, and so I think there's a case for applying your inner ear to your dialogue as much as your outer one. That is exactly what your reader will be doing when she reads your novel.

So when you first write your characters' dialogue, you should be saying it to yourself, and hearing it with your own inner ear. Ideally, all the nuances you are trying to convey should be coming through on the page, but unfortunately, it doesn't always happen as easily as that.

Saying it aloud may well make it seem more stilted than you intended, and you may wonder if you've got it right after all. Before you revise indiscriminately, always go back to your inner-ear test, and then decide how much, if any, alteration your dialogue needs.

I read a wonderful comment regarding dialogue recently. It suggested that (fictionally) every time you see a mouth, you should put words into it. Tongue-in-cheek, I think! And it all depends on which words you choose. Some mouths are just too full of them.

Chapter 8

PITFALLS OF DIALOGUE

It's perilously easy to fall into the trap of using dialogue simply to make up the suggested third of a novel. You may suddenly realise that your characters haven't spoken for a couple of pages, so you'd better give them something to say. And you do. You give them anything to relieve the monotony of the pages full of prose – isn't that what you've been told? Well, not quite.

Getting the balance of your book right is one of the things that comes with practice, including that of knowing when to include dialogue between your characters, and which type of dialogue to avoid. It also comes with knowing your characters inside out and not allowing them to annoy your readers. This can happen when you insert a bit of totally unnecessary conversation to bump up your dialogue quota.

To take this idea to extremes, for instance – a busy hotel receptionist dealing with an irate central character shouldn't launch out of the blue into a lengthy speech as to why the hotel chain needs to raise its charges to make it pay, just because your book needs a shot of dialogue in it!

The only time this scene would be acceptable would be if it had some significance on the rest of the plot. Maybe the central character is considering buying the hotel, and the receptionist's remarks serve to put him off – or to offer him a challenge. With such motivation, the comments would be valid. Standing alone, they would be padding, and the readers would be irritated by the way the girl was going off at a tangent. We do it in real life. In fiction, it should be avoided.

When to introduce dialogue into a story should ideally come through instinct and not by design. By putting yourself into your character's shoes, you should get a clearer idea of when she's ready to say something, and is not just relying on the author–narrator to tell her story. It needs to be told through her eyes, and with her words.

But balancing your novel between dialogue and narrative isn't the only pitfall for the new writer, especially one who is attempting an historical novel for the first time.

THE HISTORICAL TRAP

One of the biggest problems the first-time historical writer discovers is that of getting the characters to speak correctly for their historical period. To pepper your dialogue with 'prithees' and 'Your humble servant, Sir' and 'God's teeth' will un- doubtedly put your novel into a certain time period, but how much of such dialogue do you think your readers can take?

Historical writers tread a fine line between writing correct dialogue for the era of their stories, and the authenticity re- quired by purists and readers alike. It's advisable to use such prosaic and stiff language sparingly, while avoiding the obvi- ous mistake of letting your characters sound too modern.

I would go further. Even if an historically correct word *sounds* modern, I would avoid it. You always have choices.

Characters in your book cannot refer to things that are not in their experience yet. A young Regency lady hurrying to get ready for an evening soirée can't hitch up her skirt with a safety-pin before such things have been invented. She wouldn't be attending to such things by herself, anyway. A maid would be doing the necessary repairs.

The disadvantage of not being able to call up her friends on the telephone can delay communication between them considerably.

And is it permissible to let your medieval hero and heroine exchange an electric glance? It most certainly is not. Such gaffs will ruin a story for the reader. Research into historical and other data does not come within the scope of this book, and is covered in *How to Research your Novel* in this series.

Never was the class system more pronounced than in past times. The classes have merged far more in the twentieth century than in any other, but dialogue between fictional historical characters can exploit all stratas of society, and the pecking order between them all was very strictly observed. In a dialogue between two characters of different classes, the reader should know which is which quite clearly.

Example

> 'Missy, come quickly,' the ayah said. 'They say there is much unrest in the city, and you must get dressed and leave the house.'
>
> Her obvious agitation had the effect of making Constance more irritated than afraid, stilling her own thoughts as she moved towards the window.
>
> 'What nonsense you talk, Meera. Why should I leave the house at this ungodly hour? I've certainly no intention of doing so until my father returns from Delhi – '
>
> Even as she spoke, a stone hit the window. A sliver of glass hit Constance's arm, and she stared at the spots of blood on her soft skin. Meera's brown hand clutched at her young mistress.
>
> 'This is a bad omen, Missy. Your father's position won't help us if the law-breakers start burning – '

In that example, there are key words and phrases that establish the relationship between the two characters. The words are 'Missy' on the part of the servant, and her reference to 'Your father's position'. The girl's attitude is openly superior. 'What nonsense' and 'certainly no intention of doing so' establish this. The inclusion of less-used contemporary words, such as 'unrest', 'ungodly hour' and 'law-breakers' underline the historical flavour of the dialogue.

There is a courtliness in historical dialogue that appeals to writers and readers alike, and goes a long way towards the popularity of such books. The characters of another age share our hopes, dreams, fears and emotions, even though they express themselves differently. But they are the essence of our forefathers, and what they say adds to our insatiable curiosity about the past.

Historical novelists are well aware of the need for research into locations, dress, travel, communication, customs and so on. Inventing historical characters for your book gives you plenty of leeway for creating realistic dialogue for them. You can literally make your characters anything you want them to be, from villains to spies to dashing buccaneers. But when you put words into the mouths of actual historical persons, they should never be allowed to say things contrary to their recorded opinions.

If your political fanatic is an out-and-out socialist, then you can't have him being soft-centred towards someone with obviously conservative leanings, if researches show that he never behaved in such a way. Would Adolf Hitler have willingly entertained a Jewish gentleman to dinner?

SLANG

The use of slang words in historical and contemporary dialogue estabishes a character and a time quite effortlessly. Using the correct phraseology in the character's dialogue is a trademark of Regency novels, for instance, and the reader of Regency novels knows from the outset that conversations will be sprinkled with odd, often charming, and sometimes outrageously ridiculous phrases, because this is a part of the Regency flavour.

Ladies will sigh that they are 'melancholy' or 'feeling out of sorts', and their favourite blasphemy may well be 'fiddle-sticks'. Plans will be put 'to rout' and studious young ladies will be 'bluestockings'. The danger in writing Regency dialogue is in overdoing such phrases and words, and to throw them in at every opportunity. Your characters are still people holding conversations with one another, and if they all seem intent on making the best impression they can by their overuse of Regency slang, your writing will appear very laboured.

Slang in contemporary fiction also pin-points an era as well as a character's status. The character who refers to old so-and-so being a 'right handy little spiv' is undoubtedly in a Second World War time-setting. If a girl referred to her boyfriend as being a 'Brylcreem boy', it would set him in the RAF of the same era.

Some words used in a slang way have been used for far longer than one might think. We tend to think of 'gay' as being a modern term for mainly male homosexuality, but if a character referred to another as 'a gay woman' in 1825, she would imply that the woman led an immoral life.

It's not only in the narrative that you can make use of these slang terms, and it's usually far less clumsy to do so when the characters are talking to one another. But learn to be selective and not to overdo it. A conversation consisting of nothing but slang terms would make very tedious reading. The odd word or two among a more normal style of speaking would give the whole thing more emphasis.

An interesting exercise is to collect the number of ways in which a character might refer to a simple act, say that of sleeping. You can define status, age, lifestyle and era by the choices shown below.

'I'm just going to have a doze by the fire while I'm listening to the wireless.'

'Shush, children. Your father's having forty winks.'

'I want to take a quick nap before going into the office.'

'Methinks I shall retire to my chamber for a rest.'

'I slept like a top all night.'

'I'm feeling quite languid, Millie, and I shall take an hour's slumber. See that I'm not disturbed.'

'I feel positively soporific, Eleanor. Fetch me my shawl and leave me to drowse in the shade, there's a dear.'

'I'm flagging, Dave. I shall need some shut-eye after all this climbing.'

'I'm ready for snoresville, man.'

'The old gentleman's in the arms of Morpheus, Sir.'

'Off to sleepybyes now, darling.'

'Is the idiot out for the count?'

'I'm not sleeping, just resting my eyes.'

'It's off to dreamland with you, my girl.'

'I'm so tired, I could sleep for a week.'

'My lady is presently resting, my lord.'

'It's siesta-time . . .'

AVOIDING THE SLUSH PILE

Mention of the slush pile throws new writers into panic. If you've never heard the term before, it's what most publishers refer to as the pile of unsolicited manuscripts that come into their offices with unfailing regularity. All publishing houses have their established authors, who will obviously get a more sympathetic and faster reading than unknown ones. Being on the slush pile doesn't necessarily mean that your manuscript is awful, or that it won't get a fair reading, though the time lag between sending in a manuscript and getting a response varies enormously. It may be weeks or many months.

Don't blame the editors for that. A popular publishing house may be inundated with manuscripts and can therefore be more selective in the ones it chooses. A less commercial one may publish fewer books, so that each one has to be carefully costed before it can be taken on. Publishing is big business, but also a costly business.

So how do you avoid your manuscript being thrown out of the slush pile and arriving back on your doorstep? It's a question to which there's no single answer. Doing your homework as regards sending your work to the right publisher; keeping an eye on the market to see which books seem to be 'in' and which are currently 'out'; sending your work to an agent and relying on her vetting; being sure your background is as authentic as possible, your characters sympathetic and likeable, and your dialogue realistic.

Flaws in plotting, characterisation or dialogue will ruin your story. An editor who spots the potential in your book may suggest revisions, which you would be wise to follow through, providing you believe them to be feasible. Even an editor can be wrong when it comes to your book, but at least look at the revisions she suggests, and be prepared to compromise if necessary.

Look especially at your dialogue, and see where it can be improved. In some of the work I have been asked to assess, I have winced at some of the really bad dialogue. And never more so than in romantic novels, which brings me to:

ROMANTIC DIALOGUE

Romantic dialogue is not solely the prerogative of Mills & Boon. Any novel that contains a love story is going to need romantic dialogue to a greater or lesser degree. Characters in love do converse with one another, especially in the process of getting to know one another, which is often where the dialogue falls down.

If the author is wary of letting the couple be too friendly too soon, it often results in a sudden declaration at the end of the book, with no gradual leading-up to the finale. The readers have lost the feeling of romance that should have been filtered throughout the book, and the sense of sexual tension will be lost.

Everyone knows that romantic dialogue gets a bad press. Read out of context it can make you squirm. But it's not meant to be read aloud in that tongue-in-cheek way. It's meant to be a private conversation between two people with no eavesdroppers. To write realistic romantic dialogue, the author needs to feel sincerely about the genre, to believe in the two characters who are falling in love, and to write about them honestly and without inhibitions. This is especially true in their dialogue.

In poorly written love scenes, the characters hardly talk at all, and plenty of euphemistic narrative sets the scene and describes what the lovers are actually doing to one another. But readers have paid good money, not only to have the scenes described to them in detail, but also to hear what those lovers are saying to one another in their romantic clinches. Believe it or not, characters in romantic situations can even find humour in the situation, which can be a very refreshing reaction to editors and readers alike, providing the plot allows for such humour. Love – and sex – doesn't always have to be written in melodramatic style.

The following scene is written in light romantic style:

> Before she could stop herself, Viv had tripped over the stool and fallen headlong into his arms. The two of them crashed down on the carpet together.
>
> 'I'm sorry – ' she gasped, trying to disentangle herself and knowing what a fool she must look. To her surprise she realised he was laughing.
>
> 'What for? It's not every day a girl heads straight into my arms, and I always said you'd fall for me one of these days.'
>
> 'And I always said you were an arrogant – '
>
> The words died on her lips as she saw the teasing look in his eyes. Her hair fell around her shoulders, and she brushed it back, while making no move to get out of his arms. Why should she, when it felt so good to be here?
>
> 'We must look idiotic,' she said, starting to laugh. 'What if someone comes in?'
>
> She felt his mouth touch hers. His kiss was warm, without undue pressure, but it sent a frisson of excitement rushing through her.
>
> 'What if they do?' he retorted. 'Am I the new Managing Director or not?'
>
> 'I don't know,' she said, staring. '*Are you?*'

One of the myths about writing romantic dialogue and/or sexy scenes is that you must always include mention of body parts and/or avoid them by every possible means by those dreaded euphemisms. It's just as easy to get a charge of romance and sexual tension between the characters simply by weaving in the appropriate dialogue and action. There are also plenty of variations on describing a kiss. The following are examples from my own books:

From *Velvet Dawn* (Rowena Summers, Severn House):

> He glanced down at her, to where the once-beautiful cream silk jersey was now streaked with dirt and oil.
>
> 'You'd better take that off while I decide just what I'm going to do with you.'
>
> 'And just how is that going to help you decide?'
>
> He picked her up in his arms and strode across the room with her, kissing her with every step until they reached her bedroom.
>
> 'Someone ought to tell Fletcher the news that you're all right,' she murmured against his mouth.
>
> 'Later,' he murmured back. 'First things first.'
>
> He kicked the door shut behind them. Suddenly she wasn't tired any more.

From *Dream Lover* (Jean Innes, Zebra historical):

> 'Why are you so reluctant to say what it is you want, Breda? Didn't your father bring you up to always tell the truth?'
>
> 'Of course he did – '
>
> 'Then why won't you admit that from the moment we met, you felt something between us?'
>
> 'I was also brought up to believe that a young lady should practise modesty at all times, and not be forward.'
>
> 'I apologise,' Richard said. 'Besides, it's hardly a father's place to teach a lovely daughter the rudiments of love that I intend to teach you.'
>
> Before she could stop him she was enveloped in a dark and passionate embrace, and his mouth was hot and sweet on hers.

From *Buccaneer's Bride* (Jean Innes, Zebra historical):

'All right, you've had your funning. Now take what you want from me and go,' Sarah demanded.

'I don't want your jewels. I'm more intrigued by *you*. You seem out of place in this humdrum company. And what of your husband?' Robbie said, grinning.

'My husband was a good deal older than me. He died soon after our wedding – '

'I'm not surprised.' Robbie laughed. 'Any old fool would expire once he lost himself in such luscious surroundings.'

'You're insulting!' she snapped.

'It's no insult to tell a woman she's beautiful, nor to feel her response, no matter what her voice says.'

She was outraged. What made it worse was that all he said was true.

'I've never felt challenged by a woman before,' he said softly. 'It would be my pleasure to tame you, my lovely. I shall leave you your jewels, but I'll take this – for now.'

Before she could stop him, his mouth fastened over hers in a long, seductive kiss. She pushed him away, rubbing her hand against her mouth . . .

From *Tropical Fire* (Jean Innes, Zebra historical):

'I asked you once before if you liked what you saw,' Luke said softly. 'I ask you again, my dear Miss Rowe, because it's yours for the taking.'

She drew in her breath. He was outrageous . . . and also more exciting than any man she had ever known.

'You presume too much – ' she said, her voice hoarse.

He leaned forward to caress the side of her cheek

112

with his fingers. She shivered, feeling an almost irresistible urge to grasp those caressing fingers and bring them to her mouth. Was she going completely mad?

Wordlessly he pressed his mouth to hers. She stood as still as she could, trying very hard not to respond in the slightest way, because he was crass and undisciplined and the very epitome of bad taste.

But it was too much to expect of anyone. Pressed close to his heart, she succumbed to a wildness in her own nature that she was only just discovering . . .

HANDLING SEVERAL CHARACTERS AT ONCE

Creating dialogue between a group of characters need not be daunting. In a situation such as a party or a reunion, it's often only necessary to single out two conversationalists. It's a big mistake to try to give equal weight to everyone attending a function, just to make the room seem busy and full of people. The writing will certainly emerge as busy, but it will be muddled, with no clear-cut indication of the most important characters.

But if you want to include a small group in discussion, then the following example is from my book *A Royal Summer* (Sally Blake, Mills & Boon Masquerade). The people at the dinner party are discussing Queen Victoria's coronation that day, and all the mishaps were as historically recorded.

This also demonstrates a way of including historical fact through dialogue without making it sound like a history lesson.

'It was such a pity you missed the ceremony, my dear,' Lady Lydia said to Rosalind. 'It was very moving indeed, and so colourful too.'

Sir George sniggered. 'A bit too moving for that old buffoon Lord Rolle, Mother, wouldn't you say?'

'Shush, George, and please don't be disrespect-ful,' his mother admonished him, and turned to Rosalind and her aunt. 'What George refers to is when the old gentleman went to pay his homage to the Queen and overbalanced, falling back down the steps. The poor man is all of eighty-two years old, but when he attempted to walk up the steps again the Queen very kindly stepped down to meet him so that the incident wouldn't occur again.'

'It would have made the proceedings even longer if he'd gone back and forth all afternoon,' George said mirthfully, and according such little reverence to the day that Rosalind disliked him even more.

'But there were several awkward moments,' Celeste added, clearly as practical and unaffected by all the pomp as George. 'The Archbishop handed her the orb far too soon, and rammed the coronation ring on to the wrong finger. We heard that the poor girl almost screamed in pain at the incident, and later she had to soak her hand in cold water to remove the ring.'

'That may be, but there were some truly beauti-ful moments as well,' Lady Lydia said, clearly dis-approving of the pair of them, but too well bred to say so in company.

LOCAL ACCENTS, DIALECTS AND FOREIGN LANGUAGES

It's very tempting to pep up your characters' speeches with local accents. In small doses, it works well, but it should never be overdone. Many regional accents are completely in-decipherable to those outside the locality, and only make tedious reading when someone has to try to work through those difficult phrases. It spoils the flow of the dialogue, and holds up the enjoyment of the book, so don't overdo it. Us-ing the odd, readily acceptable regional word in the dialogue will quickly set the character in the right location, and doesn't need to be repeated in every other sentence.

Dialects are awkward to convey properly in print, and always look very hammy when the author attempts to write them down phonetically in the cause of accuracy. It's far better to leave them to the readers' imagination, and just indicate by the occasional phrase or regional word that this is a hill farmer from Wales, or a Scottish ghillie, or a London barrow-boy. Remember that a little dialect goes a long way in fiction, too much can start to resemble gibberish.

When it comes to using foreign words, my advice is to avoid them unless you're very sure of the language. If it's essential to use them, and if your characters are foreign, then you may well want to include some sentences in French or German or whatever, especially if you know these languages well. But not all readers are fluent linguists, and too much cleverness may well put them off ploughing through to the more easily understood parts of your book.

If you are uncertain of foreign languages, it's far too easy to make mistakes, especially in the idioms of another tongue, and even more so in the shortened versions of phrases that are used everyday by the locals, but which you may labour over in literal terms to try and include them in your book.

An example is the Spanish word *hay*, pronounced 'eye'. *Hay* is a most useful collective word meaning 'there is'; 'there are'; 'is there?' and 'are there?' But if you didn't know it you might end up with a horribly contrived conglomeration of words when trying to make up the simple phrase.

Foreign phrase books can be very useful for set dialogue phrases, and if you only need the occasional one or two, they may supply all that you need. But there's more to other languages than just words. People in other countries put the emphasis on different parts of their sentences from ourselves, and you need to be aware of the fact.

Spanish has no apostrophe, so they would not be able to say in Spanish 'This is my daughter's house'. They would say 'This is the house of my daughter'. A Spanish character unused to speaking in English would probably use the same phrasing, which can be quaint and charming to English ears.

THE RHYTHMS OF SPEECH

All speech has a rhythm to it, and is one of the delightful things about it. When we speak about a person's musical voice, we refer as much to what she says and the way that she says it, as to the inflexion in the voice. Indeed, one writer friend of mine once referred to the music of the words, and this seemed to sum it all up perfectly.

When you create your dialogue, keeping that sense of music in your mind will help to make your characters more appealing to the reader. If you train yourself to do it, you will hear the rhythms in your dialogue when you read it aloud. You will hear them even better when you read it to yourself, because you won't be inhibited by the sound of your own voice, which may even put you off.

A source of great frustration to beginners is the way the dialogue of published authors seems to be so natural on the written page and yet it constantly eludes them. There is no better way to get it right than by practice, and by making use of all the books that have already been published for your examples. Those authors got it right. So can you.

Chapter 9

SUMMING UP

The most satisfying way to know if your dialogue has actually worked is when readers tell you how much your characters came alive for them. What they really mean is that they saw and heard and experienced your characters' love, hate, pain and conflict. They took a vicarious pleasure in sharing all of these things with your characters, and in particular, every time they 'heard' your characters speak, they willed them on to whatever conclusion you have mapped out for them.

When you've done all you can to make your dialogue as realistic as possible, take a little longer to go through it again, to see if it can still be improved. We all want to rush our books off to a publisher, and I am no exception, but a final checking never did any manuscript any harm.

This doesn't necessarily mean endless revision. I have already expressed my views on that. Don't take the life and soul out of your writing by changing every dot and comma just for the sake of it. But do take the time to see if you have conveyed exactly the meaning you wanted, and if not, be prepared to change it. And if you've read this book so far, you should be aware of what to look out for. The following checklist might help.

ENHANCING YOUR CHARACTERS
Does your dialogue really do this for you, and have they been telling their own story?

Do you feel that you know each character more thorough-

117

ly because of the things he says, and the way that he says them?

Have you allowed one character to describe another one quite smoothly and naturally, giving the readers a useful description without stating it baldly in the narrative?

Have the emotions of your characters come through their dialogue, allowing the readers to sympathise with them, or loathe them, as the case may be?

Have you furthered the plot by the use of dialogue, especially when neatly covering the transitions of time and space?

Have you increased the sense of suspense in your story by the use of short sharp dialogue sentences where necessary?

Have you kept up the suspense in your story by means of the characters' dialogue?

Have you allowed one character to interrupt where necessary, in order to divert the other's attention from his original speech and thereby hold up the action for a while?

Have you really listened to your own characters talking?

Could you look through your manuscript pages and say at once who's talking by the strength of their dialogue?

Do your characters speak according to the way you've described them – for example, does your own version of Heathcliffe speak in a suitably strong tone and language, and not wimpishly?

MORE IMPACT THROUGH DIALOGUE

Have you carefully resisted letting your characters dwell too long on trivia, instead of getting on with the story?

Have you avoided the ping-pong effect of using too many short lines of dialogue by varying the lengths of the speeches, if only for the aesthetic look of the page?

Have you opted for too many adverbs in a dialogue scene when a few simple 'he said'/'she saids' might do?

Conversely, have you included adverbs where they help to define your meaning more accurately?

Have you checked through your big scenes to ensure that the greater part of them is told through dialogue and not simply through narrative?

Have you looked for other places in the narrative where dialogue could effectively replace certain flatter scenes?

Is there any part of the dialogue that is too weak, and could usefully be cut out?

Do your characters go on talking for too long, and become boring?

Have you written your dialogue as visually as you can, letting one character convey to another the things he has experienced as clearly as possible?

Do your child characters speak like children, without using words beyond their comprehension?

Have you adapted each character's dialogue to whoever they are speaking to at any given time?

Have you suggested your character's personality and background through his individual speech patterns?

Have you checked on the correct jargon for any particular career-oriented character?

WEAVING IN DIALOGUE AND ACTION
In any big scene such as a battle, have you brought your characters sharply into focus by their dialogue?

In any such traumatic scenes, have you allowed your characters to speak as savagely/wildly/hysterically/emotionally/rashly/blasphemously as the scene demands?

Have you let your characters tell your readers about the events they have witnessed or experienced, rather than narrating them yourself?

Even though you may be writing a deeply regional novel, have you resisted letting your characters use too many 'oh ahs' and 'ee by gums' and 'look you, boyos'?

THE FINAL PRODUCT
Let me give you a final example of dialogue, and this is written with my tongue firmly in my cheek.

'I'm thinking about writing a book, Lynn,' my sports-mad nephew said suddenly.
    'Oh yes! Last week you wanted to go to sea, and

the week before that you fancied being a film cameraman,' I said, knowing very well that he couldn't apply himself for more than ten minutes at a time to anything outside a football pitch.

Seeing his mutinous face, I softened a little. 'All right then. What kind of book are you going to write?'

'I haven't decided yet. It might be about spies, or it might be about space-ships,' he said vaguely.

'Or it might be about thinking about writing a book,' I said, grinning.

'Hey, that's not such a bad idea, brainbox. Do you think it would appeal to anybody?'

'I should think it would appeal to quite a few wannabees,' I said dryly.

'What's a wannabee?' he asked suspiciously, not sure whether or not it was something unmentionable.

'Don't you know anything?' For the life of me I couldn't resist this. 'A wannabee is somebody who wants to be something and never gets down to it. Sound familiar?'

If you caught the essence of the two characters in that small scene, then the dialogue worked. If it struck home, it worked even better ... there are probably more wannabee writers than anything else, but until they sit down and put words on paper, and submit their stories to an editor, they will never know if they can write saleable work.

All the advice given throughout this book, and the checklists given above, may seem time-consuming and tedious to someone who is starting to write fiction for the first time. But much of the expertise in writing dialogue will come by instinct, and far more will come with practise.

It's common sense to study whatever method is available for improving your craft, but in the end it must be your voice that comes through the voices of the characters you create.